Abdullah al-Udhari was born in Taiz, Yemen, in 1941. He went to schools in Taiz, Beirut, Cairo and Liverpool and read classical Arabic at London University. He has lived in London since 1962. For four years he was lecturer in Arabic at the Polytechnic of Central London. In 1974 he founded and edited *TR*, an Anglo-Arab literary and arts magazine. He has published two collections of poetry and several volumes of translations. With G. B. H. Wightman he translated *Birds through a Ceiling of Alabaster* for the Penguin Classics.

MODERN POETRY OF THE
ARAB WORLD

Translated and edited by
Abdullah al-Udhari

PENGUIN BOOKS

Penguin Books Ltd, Harmondsworth, Middlesex, England
Viking Penguin Inc., 40 West 23rd Street, New York, New York 10010, U.S.A.
Penguin Books Australia Ltd, Ringwood, Victoria, Australia
Penguin Books Canada Limited, 2801 John Street, Markham, Ontario, Canada L3R 1B4
Penguin Books (N.Z.) Ltd, 182–190 Wairau Road, Auckland 10, New Zealand

This selection first published 1986

The Acknowledgements on pages 143–50 constitute an extension of this copyright page

Filmset in Bembo (Linotron 202) by
Rowland Phototypesetting Ltd, Bury St Edmunds, Suffolk
Made and printed in Great Britain by
Cox & Wyman Ltd, Reading

For
BEIRUT

CONTENTS

Taf'ila Movement (Iraqi School): 1947–57

BADR SHAKIR AL-SAYYAB (1926–64) was born in the
village of Jaikur near Basra, Iraq. In 1944 he enrolled at
the Baghdad Teachers' Training College and after
reading Arab literature for two years switched to Eng-
lish literature, graduating in 1948. He then worked
as a schoolteacher, civil servant and journalist. In
the late forties he joined the Iraqi Communist Party,
remaining an active member until he resigned in the
mid-fifties on account of the Party's unsympathetic
approach to the Palestinian issue, Arab nationalism
and the Arab cultural heritage. As a result of his
independent views he was victimized by the Com-
munists and later by the Arab nationalists. This
persecution led to the deterioration of his health and he
died of paralysis in Kuwait. His publications include
Collected Poems (2 vols.) and *An Anthology of World
Poetry*.

NAZIK AL-MALA'IKA (1923–   ) was born in Baghdad
and educated at the Baghdad Teachers' Training
College. She teaches at Kuwait University. Her publi-
cations include *Collected Poems* (2 vols.) and three
collections of critical studies of Arab and English
poetry.

ABDUL WAHAB AL-BAYATI (1926–   ) was born in
Baghdad and educated at the Baghdad Teachers'
Training College. He was a member of the Iraqi
Communist Party for a number of years but broke

7

away on ideological grounds. He worked as a school-teacher, journalist and diplomat. He now lives in Madrid. Since the publication of his *Collected Poems* (3 vols.) he has published one further volume of poetry.

BULAND AL-HAIDARI (1926–   ) was born in Baghdad, Iraq. Self-educated, from 1963 to 1976 he lived in Lebanon, where he worked as a schoolteacher and journalist. He has lived in London since 1980. He founded and edited the short-lived London-based magazine *Arab Art*. He has published eight volumes of poetry and a collection of essays on art and literature.

Majallat Shi'r Movement (Syrian School): 1957–67

YUSUF AL-KHAL (1917–   ) was born in Tripoli, Lebanon. He read literature and philosophy at the American University of Beirut and taught there from 1944 to 1948. In the summer of 1948 he went to the USA where he worked for the United Nations and in journalism until 1955, when he returned to Beirut and resumed teaching at the American University. In 1957 he founded *Shi'r* magazine and the press Dar Majallat Shi'r, which published the work of the poets associated with the magazine. He now runs an art gallery. His publications include *Collected Poems* (1973), three plays, and translations of Carl Sandburg's *Abraham Lincoln*, T. S. Eliot's *The Waste Land*, a selection of

Robert Frost's poems, an anthology of American poetry, the New Testament and Gibran's *The Prophet*.

ADONIS (ALI AHMAD SA'ID) (1930–   ) was born in the village of Qassabin, Syria, and read literature and philosophy at Damascus University. In 1956 he settled in Lebanon and became a naturalized Lebanese. In 1968 he founded and edited the influential cultural magazine *Mawaqif*, which is the only outlet for experimental poetry in the Arab World. Since the publication of his *Collected Poems* (2 vols.) he has published three further volumes of poetry, a critical anthology of classical Arab poetry, five studies of classical and modern Arab poetry, and translations from Racine and Saint-John Perse.

UNSI AL-HAJ (1937–   ) was born in Lebanon. A former literary editor of the influential daily *An-Nahar*, he has published five collections of poetry, and translations from the *Song of Songs* and from the work of the French poets Breton, Artaud and Prévert.

CONTENTS

SHAUQI ABI SHAQRA (1935–   ) was born in Lebanon
and educated at the Hikma College, Beirut. He is the
literary editor of the daily *An-Nahar*, which he joined
in 1964. He has published five collections of poetry,
and translations from the work of Rimbaud and Apol-
linaire.

FU'AD RIFQA (1930–   ) was born in Syria and educated at
the American University of Beirut and Tübingen
University, Germany. He lived for a time in the USA,
but is now a naturalized Lebanese and lectures at the
American University of Beirut. His publications in-
clude five volumes of poetry, a collection of philo-
sophical essays, and two selections of translations
from the poems of Rilke and Hölderlin.

MUHAMMAD AL-MAGHUT (1932–   ) was born in Sala-
miya, Syria, and lives in Damascus. Self-educated, he
works as a journalist and writes for television and the
cinema. He has written three volumes of poetry and
two plays.

JABRA IBRAHIM JABRA (1919–) was born in Beth-
lehem, studied at the Arab College, Jerusalem, and
read English literature at Fitzwilliam House, Cam-
bridge. He has lived in Iraq since 1948 and is a natural-
ized Iraqi citizen. He has written novels, short stories,
criticism on art and literature, and three volumes of
poetry. His translations include *Hamlet*, *King Lear*,
Faulkner's *The Sound and the Fury*, two volumes of
Frazer's *The Golden Bough* and Wilson's *Axel's Castle*.

TAUFIQ SAYIGH (1923–71) was born in Syria and spent
his childhood in Tiberias, Palestine. A contemporary
of Jabra Ibrahim Jabra at the Arab College in Jeru-
salem, he studied at the American University of Beirut
and taught at Pembroke College, Cambridge, and at
the School of Oriental and African Studies, London.
In 1961 he founded and edited the magazine *Hiwar*, the
Arab counterpart of *Encounter*, which folded in 1966
following the scandal caused by the revelation that
Encounter had been funded by the CIA. From 1968
until his death in 1971 he was a visiting lecturer at the
University of California at Berkeley. His publications
include three volumes of poetry and translations of T.
S. Eliot's *Four Quartets* and of a selection of American
poetry.

RIAD AL-RAYYES (1937–) was born in Damascus,
Syria. He read economics at the Cambridgeshire
Technical College and School of Arts, Cambridge,
and now lives in London, working as a journalist and
business consultant. He was the London editor of *Shi'r*
magazine, and has published two collections of poetry
and a critical study of modern Arab poetry.

CONTENTS

RASHID HUSSEIN (1936–77) was born in the village of
Musmus, Palestine. He went to school in Nazareth
and worked as a schoolteacher and journalist before
leaving Israel for the USA in 1966. He was persecuted
by both the Arabs and the Israelis for his belief in
Israeli–Palestinian co-existence. He took to drinking
and died in a fire in his New York flat. His publications
include three volumes of poetry, a selection of Chaim
Bialic's poems and a Hebrew translation of Palestinian
folk poems.

MU'IN BESSEISSO (1926–84) was born in Gaza and
studied at Cairo University, afterwards working as a
schoolteacher, broadcaster and journalist. He died of a
heart attack in a London hotel. He wrote seven
volumes of poetry, a number of plays and three auto-
biographical prose works. Some of his poems were
translated into Russian by Yevtushenko, and the Rus-
sian version of 'Traffic Lights' was set to music.

SALAH NIAZI (1935–   ) was born in Nasiriya, Iraq, and
educated at the Baghdad Teachers' Training College
and the School of Oriental and African Studies, Lon-
don. He has lived in London since 1963 and worked
for the BBC Arabic Service from 1965 to 1984. He
has published five volumes of poetry.

Beirut Experience: 1982–

KHALIL HAWI (1925–82) was born in Shuwair, Lebanon,
and educated at the American University of Beirut and
Pembroke College, Cambridge. He was Professor of

Arab literature at the American University of Beirut, and the author of five collections of poems. He committed suicide following Israel's invasion of Lebanon in June 1982. 'Lebanon' is one of the last poems he wrote before he died.

SAMI MAHDI (1940–   ) was born in Baghdad, Iraq. A professional journalist, he has published six collections of poems.

SA'DI YUSUF (1934–   ) was born in Basra, Iraq, and educated at the Baghdad Teachers' Training College. A former member of the Iraqi Communist Party, he was in Beirut during Israel's invasion of Lebanon in 1982. He now lives in Cyprus. His first poem appeared in the first issue of *Shi'r* magazine. Since the publication of his *Collected Poems* in 1978 he has published three more volumes of poetry.

MAHMOUD DARWISH (1942–   ) was born in the village of al-Barweh, Palestine. He worked as a journalist in Haifa until he left Israel in 1971 for Beirut, where he remained until 1982. He now lives in Paris and edits the magazine *Al-Karmal*. He was awarded the Lotus Prize in 1969 and the Lenin Prize in 1983.

CONTENTS

INTRODUCTION

A reading of Arab poetry from the last hundred years reveals two distinct developments. Firstly, there are poets who felt that the outworn poetic tools were no longer capable of adequately conveying their responses to the social issues of their day. These turned to classical poetry for inspiration. They looked for periods which paralleled their own and then explored the various techniques by which the classical poets registered their concern. Secondly, there are those poets who have successfully managed to blend classical Arab tradition with European modernism.

Among the first category was a group of poets based in Egypt known as the Revivalists, who were prominent at the end of the nineteenth century. They rejected the poetry of their immediate predecessors, turning instead to classical poetry and looking for poems that idealized the situations and qualities their age lacked. Emotionally and intellectually they were overwhelmed by the splendour of the past; writing about it became a form of escape from their wretched times. As they shuttled through different periods, the Revivalists wrote fine poems in imitation of major poets like Nabigha al-Dhubiani (535–604), Abu Tammam (788–845), Mutanabbi (915–65) and Ibn Zaidun (1003–70). In other words their poetry remained within a sphere dominated by a classical mentality.

In the early part of this century another group of poets known as the Mahjaris ('Emigrants') emerged from the Lebanese, Syrian and Palestinian communities settled in the USA and Latin America. Their aim was to preserve their identity and to overcome the culture-shock they suffered in their new environments. So they turned to classical poetry. But, feeling a greater sense of urgency for change than the Revivalists, they looked for elements of tension resulting from the clash of values in societies undergoing change. They took up the argument of the Abbasid poets that poets should write about their times in everyday speech. It is not surprising that Abbasid poets like Abu Nuwas (762–813), Ibn al-Mu'tazz (861–908), Ma'arri (973–1057), the Sufi Ibn al-Farid (1181–1234) and the Andalusian *muwashaha*[1] poets appealed to them. Their attempts to modernize Arab poetry culminated in the emergence of two poetry movements, Arrabita al-Qalamiya ('The Pen Bond'), founded in

---

1. A poem in several stanzas with a varied rhyming structure.

17

1920 in New York and led by Gibran Kahlil Gibran, and Al-Usba al-Andalusia ('The Andalusian Group'), formed in São Paulo in 1933. The Mahjari poets created a new diction, new metaphors and new rhythms, and developed new forms based on the Abbasid and *muwashaha* forms.

Arrabita poets' plan was to start a press which would publish the work of its group and a magazine to propagate their revolutionary ideas about classical poetry and the kind of poetry they were writing. They stressed the importance of translating works from other languages as a way of injecting fresh blood into their language.

The New York poets Ameen Rihani (1876–1940) and Gibran Kahlil Gibran (1883–1931), who wrote in both Arabic and English, stand out as the most inventive of the Mahjari poets. Indeed it is from them that modern Arab poetry traces its descent. With Rihani and Gibran Arab poetry ceased to be a description of reality as seen through a window and expressed in a received language. They revived the Jahili (pre-Islamic) and Sufi concept of the poet as a visionary, and introduced two new poetic forms which Rihani called *shi'r manthur*[2] (free verse) and *qasidat al-nathr* (prose poem). The innovations of Rihani and Gibran brought an element of excitement into Arab poetry.

In 1911 Rihani published his second volume of *Rihaniyat* which contained essays, speeches and ten *shi'r manthur* poems.[3] In a brief introduction to the poems Rihani intimated that the idea of the *shi'r manthur* was suggested by Walt Whitman's 'free verse', which he translated as *shi'r hur* and described as having its own particular rhythm produced by the employment of different metres within the poem. The appearance of these poems by Rihani was a turning point in the history of Arab poetry. In them he abandoned the predominant *bait* (distich) structure, which consisted of two hemistiches with corresponding equal numbers of feet and the same rhyming letter falling at the end of the second hemistich throughout the poem, using instead the neglected single *shatr* (hemistich). His stanzas are irregular, the lines varying in length, with no metre and an irregular rhyming scheme like that of Qur'anic verse. His diction and rhythm are those of natural speech and his imagery pastoral and homely:

2. It is interesting to note that Al-Shabushti (d. 1008) says in his book *Al-Dayarat* ('The Monasteries') that the Abbasid Caliph Al-Mu'tamid (d. 892) wrote *shi'r ghair mawzun* (poetry without metre).

3. Rihani's first *shi'r manthur* poem was printed in the magazine *Al-Hilal* in 1905.

> I feel an intense pleasure seeing these
>   new buds growing.
> I've counted them many times like a mother
>   counting the teeth of her little boy.

In 1923 Rihani published thirteen more *shi'r manthur* poems[4] with a manifestly down-to-earth message:

> I am the East.
> I have philosophies, I have religions, who
>   would exchange them for airplanes?

Rihani introduced into his poetry mythological and Christian themes, and metaphors – for instance, the cross, wound, lily, river, forest, lark, tourist, jasmine, homeland – which became trade-marks of modern Arab poetry.

Gibran's major contribution to Arab poetry is his revolutionary attitude to the establishment and to language. He brutally attacked the hypocrisy and corruption of the political, religious and social order of his day. He also injected a new force and resonance into language.

The generation of poets who followed Rihani and Gibran did not develop the potential of *shi'r manthur* and *qasidat al-nathr*, but wrote poems in conventional forms and sentimental diction reminiscent of late Romantic and late Symbolist poetry.

Since the late 1940s modern poets have faced problems far greater than the ones encountered by the Mahjari poets. While the latter wrote about their experiences as aliens in foreign countries, the modern poets had to contend with being alienated in their own countries. The Mahjari poets observed their home world from the outside; the modern poets saw it from within, and noticed the cracks in the wall. They witnessed their countries being ravaged by *coups d'état*, wars and civil wars. Like the Mahjari poets they went back to their classical poetic heritage, but they brought to it a broader and sharper insight. They also built upon the experiments of the Mahjari poets, especially those of Rihani and Gibran.

Since the late forties modern Arab poetry has been dominated by four major trends: the Taf'ila ('foot') Movement (also known as the Shi'r Hur Movement), the Majallat Shi'r Movement (based on *Shi'r* magazine), the Huzairan ('June') Experience, and the Beirut Experience.

---

4. These formed part of the fourth volume of *Rihaniyat*.

TAF'ILA MOVEMENT (IRAQI SCHOOL): 1947–57

In 1947 Nazik al-Mala'ika and Badr Shakir al-Sayyab published two experimental poems which became the starting point of modern Arab poetry in general and the Taf'ila Movement in particular. The two poems had irregular lines and an irregular rhyming scheme. Apart from the metrically controlled beat, the form of the two poems follows the pattern of Rihani's *shi'r manthur*. Their composition represented an act of defiance against established poetic values.

In 1949 Al-Mala'ika published her second collection *Shrapnel and Ashes*, which included several *taf'ila* poems together with her first experimental poem, published two years earlier in a literary magazine in Beirut. In the introduction Al-Mala'ika argued that the current forms had been exhausted and were incapable of encapsulating the contemporary poet's experiences, born of the events that engulfed the Arab world after the Second World War. She emphasized that the *taf'ila bait*, which could be of one or any number of feet, gave the poet a greater freedom of movement, enabling him to dispense with unnecessary padding.

By the mid-fifties Al-Mala'ika, Al-Sayyab, Abdul Wahab al-Bayati and Buland al-Haidari had created more flexible forms and had freed poetry from the sentimental indulgence of the escapist poetry of the thirties and early forties.

The association of Al-Sayyab and Al-Bayati with the Iraqi Communist Party helped to sharpen their awareness of the political and social problems of Iraq. Their primary preoccupation was that their poetry should reflect the concerns of ordinary people. They strove to write in a language which was immediate, but without compromising its poetic strength. Because of their political commitment Al-Sayyab and Al-Bayati suffered persecution and exile, treatment which only strengthened their resolve. This is exemplified by Al-Sayyab's poem 'Rain Song', written in 1953 while he was in exile in Kuwait, in which he describes the abuses of power in Iraq. When the poem was published in the magazine *Al-Adab* in Beirut in 1954, it put the Taf'ila Movement on the map and established Al-Sayyab as the leading poet of his generation.

'Rain Song' is the first modern *taf'ila* poem to have popular appeal throughout the Arab world. Its success lies in the poet's ability to harmonize classical and *taf'ila* techniques. Al-Sayyab demonstrated that it is possible to use classical diction and metaphors to speak of contemporary issues:

Every tear of the starved who have no rags to their backs
Every drop of blood shed by a slave
Is a smile awaiting fresh lips
Or a nipple glowing in the mouth of a newborn
In tomorrow's youthful world, giver of life.

His use of the conjunction 'or' to emphasize a particular image (Your eyes are palm groves refreshed by dawn's breath / Or terraces the moon leaves behind.) betrays the influence of the Mujamhara poem of the pre-Islamic poet Abid Ibn al-Abras (d. 555).[5] The use of the conjunction 'and' and the comparative 'like' as an indispensable link between a series of images is a technique employed by classical poets, especially Ibn al-Mu'tazz. Further, 'rain' itself is a potent image in classical literature, where it is associated with the rise and fall of civilizations. Classical influence is also evident in Al-Bayati's poem 'To Ernest Hemingway'. Superficially it appears that Al-Bayati is imitating Lorca, but in actual fact he is employing the classical 'jump-cut' technique which, without warning, suddenly shifts the poem from one experience to another, from direct to indirect speech and from one emotion to another.

MAJALLAT SHI'R MOVEMENT (SYRIAN SCHOOL): 1957–67

When Yusaf al-Khal returned to Lebanon from the USA in 1955, he realized that there was no publication dedicated entirely to modern poetry. He therefore decided to start a magazine and a press devoted to publishing the work of modern poets, along the lines of Arrabita. In 1956 he brought together a number of young poets whose aim was to revolutionize Arab poetry like the Arrabita poets, and in January 1957 launched the press Dar Majallat Shi'r and the quarterly *Shi'r* magazine. The Shi'r poets included Yusuf al-Khal, Al-Sayyab, Adonis, Unsi al-Haj, Shauqi Abi Shaqra, Fu'ad Rifqa, Muhammad al-Maghut, Jabra Ibrahim Jabra, Tawfiq Sayigh, Khalil Hawi, Riad al-Rayyes, Isam Mahfouz, Sa'di Yusuf and others. The Taf'ila poets Al-Mala'ika and Al-Haidari were also regular contributors to *Shi'r* magazine. The Shi'r

5. The Mujamhara poems are seven Jahili (pre-Islamic) poems singled out by the classical critic Abu Zaid al-Qurashi (d. 787) as among the finest of their period, despite the fact that they are not numbered among the seven Mu'allaqat ('suspended') poems considered pre-eminent by the Jahili poets themselves. Chosen in competition, the Mu'allaqat are said to have been written out in gold and put on display (hence 'suspended') in the Ka'ba, Mecca. To be eligible, poems had to adhere strictly to a given form; Al-Abras's Mujamhara poem would have been disqualified by the very metrical variety which gives it such interest for modern poets.

poets adopted the revolutionary ideas on poetry of the great socio-political and literary critic Antun Sa'ada. In his critical work *Cultural Conflict in Syrian Literature*, Sa'ada held that poetry should not only reflect political and social realities but should also project a 'vision' of the future. Sa'ada suggested that modern poets should create their own idiom, forms and images, and that they should exploit the traditions of the civilizations that flourished in the area before Islam. He encouraged poets to use historical and mythological themes to interpret contemporary situations. He also advised them to evaluate this classical poetic heritage and to link its positive aspects with the positive elements of other cultures. Sa'ada founded the Syrian Social Nationalist Party in 1932. He believed in the unity of the Greater Syria, which included Syria, Lebanon, Iraq and Palestine. His ideas, as well as those of Rihani and Gibran, formed the back-bone of the Shi'r Movement and were amplified by Al-Khal, Adonis, Al-Haj and Al-Sayyab. Sa'ada's last words before he was killed by the Lebanese authorities in 1949, 'My death is my victory', were echoed by Al-Sayyab in his poem 'River and Death' as 'My death is a victory'.

The Shi'r poets developed *shi'r manthur* and *qasidat al-nathr* but, unlike Rihani's, their *shi'r manthur* lacked the feature of rhyme. Rihani's and Gibran's influences are evident in the work of Al-Khal, Adonis, Al-Maghut, Al-Haj, Al-Sayyab and Al-Bayati.

Most of the Shi'r poets are Christian, and writing from this viewpoint, they broadened the scope of Arab poetry. For the first time Arab readers gained an insight into another culture. The poetry of Al-Khal, for instance, projects a Christian metaphysical experience. Rifqa, on the other hand, introduces a Christian view of contemporary issues, while Shaqra describes the ordinary life of Lebanese Christians living in mountain villages.

Al-Khal's intellectual discipline, Adonis's imaginative drive, Al-Haj's aggressive tone, Shaqra's stinging humour and Al-Maghut's ironic thrust became the distinguishing features of the Shi'r Movement.

Al-Khal's and Adonis's verse established a link with Abbasid poetry (750–1258) by reflecting the constant efforts of Abbasid poets to convey personal attitudes in new forms. (Incidentally, it is interesting to note that some of the innovations of the late Abbasid poets are remarkably similar to the experiments of twentieth-century poets. They include cut-up poems, sound poems, concrete poems and palindrome poems. Saladin's Vizier Al-Qadi al-Fadil (1135–1200) wrote an experimental poem of 24 distiches of which the first hemistich is in prose followed by a second hemistich in verse, a sequence repeated throughout the poem. Al-Khal propounded that the *bait* should function like a paragraph – that is, that the idea expressed in the *bait* is contained within it. Adonis revived the neglected *qit'a* (short poem) form and explored classical themes, as in 'The New Noah', which is based on Ma'arri's poem 'The earth longs for the flood / To cleanse it of its dirt'.

The Shi'r poets have been responsible for radically changing people's views on classical and modern poetry, language, translation and religion. Their ability to fuse classical techniques with Symbolist, Modernist, Futurist, Imagist, Dada and Surrealist theories on poetry is one of their main achievements and represents a historic literary advance.

Shi'r magazine also played an active role in introducing the work of major American and European poets to Arab readers. It ceased publication in 1964, reappeared in 1967 and then finally folded in 1970.

HUZAIRAN EXPERIENCE: 1967–82

Israel's sweeping victory over the Arab armies in the Huzairan (June) War of 1967 stunned the Arab world. The August 1967 issue of the magazine *Al-Adab* printed Nizar Qabbani's poem 'Footnotes to the Book of the Setback', which captured the mood of a nation shattered by defeat. The poem was banned throughout the Arab world, and as a result was smuggled into every Arab country, printed surreptitiously and learnt by heart. It released a flood of political frustration and anger that found expression in what is now known as Al-Adab al-Huzairani ('The June Literature').

The disillusioned Arab people found that the poetry of the newly emerged Palestinian poets like Mahmoud Darwish, Samih al-Qasim and Rashid Hussein expressed their aspirations. These poets who were living in Israel regarded writing poetry as the only way of asserting their Arab identity within an alien culture and are known as the Resistance Poets.

Poets believed at the time that the 1967 war had exposed the moral bankruptcy of the Arab establishment. This view is effectively summed up in Samih al-Qasim's poem, 'Sons of War':

> On his wedding night
> They took him to war.
>
> Five years of hardship.

One day he returned
On a red stretcher
And his three sons
Met him at the port.

The partial victory of the Arab armies in the Arab–Israeli War of
October 1973 gave new credibility to their leaders. The two wars evoked
a sense of unified Arab identity which associated itself with a common
cultural heritage. However, this new unity tended to create instability
within Arab states as their citizens began to regard themselves as Arabs
first and nationals of a particular state only second. In order to consolidate
their regimes the national leaders pursued a policy of breaking up the
Arab cultural heritage into separate entities. Pre-Islamic poets like Imru
al-Qais (d. 542) and Umayyad poets like Umar Ibn Abi Rabi'a (644–711)
became 'Saudi poets'. Abbasid poets like Abu Nuwas and Mutanabbi
'Iraqi poets', Abu Tammam and Ma'arri 'Syrian poets', and so on.
Nevertheless, the Huzairan poets continue to seek inspiration from the
classical past, in which they see a world where Arab culture was whole.

BEIRUT EXPERIENCE: 1982–

In June 1982 Israel invaded Lebanon and occupied Beirut. This was the
first time Israel had occupied an Arab capital. The destruction of Beirut
had a devastating effect on Arab culture.

Three dominant images appear in the poetry written during the Israeli
occupation. These are the street, the desert and the sea. Sa'di Yusuf
sketches street scenes of Beirut under siege. Adonis's poem 'The Desert'
is a description of a civilized city reduced to rubble. The elimination of
the city results in the return of the desert, which in the poem becomes a
place of purification and meditation, signifying a return to the roots.

The sea image recurs in Darwish's latest poems, where it symbolizes
the temporary home of the Palestinians in the diaspora. His 'Brief
Reflections on an Ancient and Beautiful City on the Coast of the
Mediterranean Sea' was written after the PLO had left Beirut, while the
last seven poems in this collection were written when the PLO forces
were leaving Tripoli. A note of desperation pervades these poems. They
are unique snapshots of Palestinian vulnerability. This was the first time a
Palestinian poet had taken the Palestinian leaders to task for selling false
hopes to their people. For Darwish, Israel's invasion of Lebanon showed

the lack of ideological direction of the Palestinian leadership: 'We have a country of words. Speak speak so we may know the end of this travel.'

In the future historians will come to appreciate the unique role Beirut has played in the cultural life of the Arabs. Poets from Egypt, Iraq, Syria and other Arab countries used to seek refuge in Beirut, where they could publish their works without fear of censorship. To poets, Beirut symbolized the unity of Arab culture. Over the years politicians have succeeded in breaking up the Arab World into different political states but failed to sustain each of them by a credible cultural identity. As a result the powers-that-be considered Beirut a threat to their regimes. Therefore they destroyed it, silenced the poets and forced most of them to return to their home countries. Each government hoped the return of the exiled poets would encourage the resident ideologically orientated poets to develop separate regional languages in contrast to the common Arab language as we understand it.

The strength of the Arab poet is that he writes about the misery and tragedy of individuals who suffer the effects of politicians obsessed with the old illusions of grandeur. The politician proclaims nationalism and promotes sectional interests. The poet proclaims the individual and promotes Arab dignity. One broadcasts propaganda, the other writes the truth. It follows that Arab poetry is a high-risk business.

It will be interesting to see whether the new poetry will come from poets who consider themselves citizens of a particular Arab country or from poets writing as representatives of a single ancient but revitalized, dynamic tradition.

> This is the age of monkeys
> You might as well obey them
> *Abu Nuwas* (762–813)

EDITOR'S NOTE

To avoid misunderstanding, I should point out that a few poems have been edited with the approval of the poets concerned.

I should like to express my gratitude to John Heath-Stubbs and George Wightman for their advice, suggestions and encouragement.

TAF'ILA MOVEMENT

BADR SHAKIR AL-SAYYAB

Rain Song

Your eyes are palm groves refreshed by dawn's breath
Or terraces the moon leaves behind.
When your eyes smile the vines flower
And the lights dance
Like the moon's reflections on a river
Gently sculled at the crack of dawn
Like stars pulsating in the depth of your eyes
That sink in mists of grief like the sea
Touched by the evening's hands
And wrapped in winter warmth and autumn shiver,
Death and birth, dark and light.

A fit of tears, a shot of joy reaching the sky
Sweep my soul
Like the thrill of a boy frightened by the moon
Like a rainbow that sips the clouds
Then melts in the rain . . .
And the children giggle in the vineyards,
And the rain song
Tickles the silence of the birds
In trees . . .
Rain . . .
Rain . . .
Rain . . .
The evening yawns and the clouds
Go on pouring their loaded tears
Like a little boy raving about his mother
He's not seen since he awoke a year ago
And is told: 'She'll be back the day after tomorrow . . .'
She has to come back,
Though his chums murmur she's over there
Asleep in a grave on the side of the hill
Licking soil and drinking rain
Like a sad fisherman pulling in his nets,

Cursing the water and fate,
Scattering his song as the moon recedes.
Rain . . .
Rain . . .
Do you know what sadness the rain brings?
And how the gutters burst into sobs when it pours?
And how lost the lonely feel?
Incessant – like running blood, like the hungry,
Like love, like children, like the dead – is the rain.
Your eyes float around me when it rains.
With the shells and the stars across the waves of the Gulf
Lightning sweeps Iraq's beaches
As they turn into sunrise
But the night draws a blanket of blood over them.
I roar at the Gulf: 'Gulf,
Giver of pearls, shells and death!'
And the echo rings back
In sobs:
'Gulf,
Giver of shells and death . . .'

I can almost hear Iraq collecting and storing
Thunders and lightnings on plains and mountains,
And when the men snap their seal
The winds leave no trace
Of Thamud in the wadi.
I can almost hear palm trees drinking rain,

Thamud: The Thamudis or Thamudenese of Ptolomy and Pliny were an ancient Arab people who lived in Wadi al-Qura in Northern Arabia. The legend goes that the Thamudis, who spent their summers in palaces in the plains and their winters on the mountains in homes hewn into the mountains like those of Petra, worshipped seventy gods. This faith displeased God and He sent them a prophet called Salih to show them the right path. For over a hundred years the Thamudis mocked Salih. One day they challenged him to prove himself a prophet by a miracle. In response to Salih's prayer God sent a shiver through the mountain, and the mountain gave birth to a red, pregnant she-camel. Salih told the Thamudis to let the she-camel graze freely, and that she would drink water for one day and provide them with milk on the next day. He also warned them that if the she-camel were killed God would punish them. The Thamudis disregarded the warning and killed the she-camel. The outraged prophet told the Thamudis that within the next three days their faces would turn yellow, red and black. Then they would all die. The Thamudis did not take him seriously. But when they saw their faces changing colour, they knew they were doomed. God sent the angel Gabriel, who let out a cry which ripped their hearts and burst their ears and killed them instantly. A fire came down from heaven and burnt them.

Villages crying, emigrants
Struggling with oars and sails
Against Gulf storms and thunders and singing:
'Rain . . .
Rain . . .
Rain . . .
There is famine in Iraq:
People watch the corn harvests thrown
To the crows and locusts
And grinders pounding
Grains and stones in the fields
Rain . . .
Rain . . .
Rain . . .
To avoid suspicion on departure night
We hide our tears under the rain . . .
Rain . . .
Rain . . .
Since we were children
The sky has slipped into clouds in winter
And it always rained.
Every year the soil grows into leaf
Yet we're hungry.
In Iraq not a year has passed without famine.
Rain . . .
Rain . . .
Rain . . .
Every drop of rain
Holds a red or yellow flower.
Every tear of the starved who have no rags to their backs
Every drop of blood shed by a slave
Is a smile awaiting fresh lips
Or a nipple glowing in the mouth of a newborn
In tomorrow's youthful world, giver of life!
Rain . . .
Rain . . .
Rain . . .
And Iraq springs into leaf in the rain . . .'

I roar at the Gulf: 'Gulf,
Giver of pearls, shells and death!'
And the echo rings back
In sobs:
'Gulf,
Giver of shells and death.'
The Gulf casts its abundant gifts on the sand:
Foam, shells and the bones of an emigrant
Who drank death
At the bottom of the Gulf.
In Iraq a thousand serpents drink liqueur of flowers
Reared on Euphrates's dew.
I hear an echo
Ringing in the Gulf:
'Rain . . .
Rain . . .
Rain . . .
Every drop of rain
Holds a red or yellow flower.
Every tear of the starved who have no rags to their backs
Every drop of blood shed by a slave
Is a smile awaiting fresh lips
Or a nipple glowing in the mouth of a newborn
In tomorrow's youthful world, giver of life.'

It is still raining.

The River and Death

Buwaib . . .
Buwaib . . .
Tower bells lost at the bottom of the sea,
Water in the jars, sunset on the trees,
Jars overspill with rain bells
Whose crystal melts in the call
'Buwaib . . . Buwaib'.

Buwaib: A river in Jaikur.

Longing for you races in my blood,
Buwaib, my sad rain.
I wish I could walk in the dark
Bearing a year's longing on each finger
As if I were bringing you gifts
Of wheat and flowers.
I wish I could go over the hill
To see the moon
Coursing through your banks, planting shadows
And filling baskets
With water, fish and flowers.
I wish I could follow the moon through you
And hear pebbles rattling in your depth
Like thousands of birds in trees.
Are you a forest of tears or a forest of a river?
The unsleeping fish, do they sleep at daybreak?
The stars, do they go on waiting,
Threading silk through thousands of needles?
Buwaib,
I wish I could plunge in you to pick up shells
To build a home
And switch on the moon and the stars
To light the greenness of the water and the trees.
At low tide in the morning I'd sail through you to the sea
For death is the children's spellbound world
And you, Buwaib, are its hidden door.

2

Buwaib . . . Buwaib,
Twenty years have gone.
Each year has been a lifetime.
At nightfall
I lie sleepless in bed
My conscience strained like a tree whose branches,
Birds and fruit weigh until daybreak.
The grieved world moves my blood and tears like rain.
My death bells are ringing in my veins,
My longing for a bullet's coldness ripping my breast
Like hell burning bones

Races in my blood.
I wish I could drown in my blood
To share humanity's burden
And bring back life. My death is a victory.

Shadows of Jaikur

Jaikur, your shadows of palm trees
Are as fresh as the dawn
Rising over the clouds and water sleeping on a beach.
Your shadows are like the eyelashes of a boy tired of playing.
I wish my eyes were jetting the moonlight of your fountain
So I could feel the shiver of a dream springing in my soul.
You are a fountain of shadows, of flowers and birds.

Jaikur, your shadows are springs running in my mind,
Watering my thirsty soul.
Under your shadows
I dream of travelling, of the wind and the sea.
With the high waves your shadows light the eyes of swordfish
Like fragments of a falling star,
Like the lamps of the dead in the hands of mermaids.

Jaikur, pick up my bones,
Shake the dust off my shroud
And in the stream
Cleanse my heart, a window opening to fire.
My country, had it not been for you
My strings would have found no wind to carry my sighs and poems;
Had it not been for you
God's face wouldn't have been my fate.

Jaikur: Al-Sayyab's village near Basra.

NAZIK AL-MALA'IKA

New Year

New Year, don't come to our homes,
We are echoes from a ghost world.
People have dropped us,
Night and the past have slipped from us,
Fate has forgotten us.
Drained of longing, drained of hope,
We have no memory, no dream:
Our calm faces have lost their colour,
Lost their spark.
We flinch from time to nothingness,
Unaware of the stings of regret,
We just go on living in soft palaces.

New Year, move on,
There's no chance for us to wake:
Our veins are made of reed,
Anger has stopped flowing in our blood.
Who said the soul may explode?
I wish we were dead and rejected by the graves.
If only we could measure time by the years
If only we knew what it is to belong to a place
If only we were afraid of madness
If only travelling could disrupt our lives
If only we could die like other people.

ABDUL WAHAB AL-BAYATI

The Fugitive

I dreamt I was a fugitive
Hiding in a forest.
The wolves in a distant country
Hounded me through black deserts and over rough hills.
My dear, our separation was torture.
I dreamt I was without a home,
Dying in an unknown city,
Dying alone, my love, without a home.

The Arab Refugee

I

Ants gnaw his flesh
Crows peck his flesh
The Arab refugee nailed to the cross.

The Arab refugee
Begs and spends his nights in railway stations
Crying his eyes out.
And Jaffa is just a small label
On a box of oranges.

2

Stop knocking on my door
There's no life left in me.
And Jaffa is just an orange label
It leaves the dead undisturbed.

3

They've sold the memory of Saladin
They've sold his horse and shield
They've sold the grave of refugees.

4

Who would buy an Arab refugee for a loaf of bread?
My blood is running dry
But you go on laughing.
I am Sinbad
I store my treasures in your children's hearts.

Ants gnaw his flesh
Crows peck his flesh
The Arab refugee begging at your door.

Hamlet

Don't bring the curtain down
I am Hamlet without a mask
Blowing up the secrets
Don't interrupt
I am dying
Don't laugh you evil people
I've just played one of the most tragic parts
Don't interrupt
The tide of the world's stage
Sweeps me away
Don't laugh
Stop the tide
Don't purse your lips
Don't turn off the lights
I feel dizzy
I am dying
Don't laugh
Don't touch me you evil people
I am Hamlet
My blood stains the walls
Don't interrupt

I am Hamlet without a mask
Swept by the tide
Across the rivers
Beyond the lines of the small stage and the curtains

An Apology for a Short Speech

Ladies and gentlemen
My speech is short
I'd hate to let words take up my time.
My tongue
Is not a wooden sword.
My words, ladies, are golden,
My words, gentlemen, are grapes of wrath.
I'm not drunk, just tired.
The candles flicker out,
The nights get colder.
I carry my heart in a briefcase,
Like a dead child,
Through thousands of betrayals and cheap lies.
My speech was short,
And I'm not drunk, just playing my suffering.
I'm not a caesar:
Rome is burning.
My soul is suffocated
By thousands of betrayals and cheap lies.
Goodbye
Ladies and gentlemen.

To Ernest Hemingway

I

In Spain

Death in Madrid
Blood in the veins
Daisies under your feet and snow
The fiestas of Spain are without processions
The grief of Spain is without end
For whom these bells toll?
Lorca is silent
Blood in a rose bowl
And the night of Granada is dying under Civil Guards' hats and iron

The children in the cradle
Are crying
Lorca is silent
And you in Madrid
Your weapon: anguish
Words and a live volcano
For whom these bells toll?
You are silent
Blood spattered on the bed the forests and the sierras

2

On The Verge Of Death

Fire in the smoke
Wine in the leather bottle the rose in the garden
Syllables birds lovesickness and time
The silence of the seas disturbs the crew
And once upon a time
There was a bloody struggle between the forces of darkness and man
It's eight o'clock
Tonight we'll meet in the garden of forgetfulness!
And he disappeared in the streets of an unknown city
A girl sobbed
Two eyes closed
I lost him
I found him in the books of Spanish travellers
He used to sing under the banner of the earth's people
Under the banner of man

3

The End

Death
Lorca told me
And the moon told me
You lost me
The guitar string lost you
Boredom killed you
You departed when spring was coming

The gypsies have struck camp
Their tents were burnt
Their flowers were burnt
A song bleeding
It was the moon told me fate's ordinance
I asked Shaikh Muhyiddin after you
He said: there is a stone in my mouth
Divine love and your idol are under the moon's feet
The massacres of the world are in your heart the ruins and the
    memory
My friend Shaikh Muhyiddin told me
Don't ask for news
People go and never return
The secret died on our lips

Profile of the Lover of the Great Bear

I

When he returned from his travels
I used to see him at night
Walking under the snow
His head bent, alone,
And when you called him
His reply, a vague smile
Fading in the wind and the dark
And within himself he resumed his daily torment and the quest
For love's continent
Buried under the snow and screams
Shaking in his long overcoat on the white pavement
As though a thousand years had passed him by and within himself
He was burning travelling or returning
Waiting for a new sign to appear in the black sky
Or a spark in the unknown

2

He was a comet bleeding
Returned from his travels and burnt out

Shaikh Muhyiddin: Known as Ibn al-Arabi (1164–1240); an Andalusian Sufi poet.

3
When he returned I never knew whence he came
And where he'd been the spellbound

4
I used to see him
And when you called him, his reply, a vague smile
Fading in the light and the dark

BULAND AL-HAIDARI

The Postman

Postman,
What do you want?
I've kept away from the world.
You've made a mistake . . .
        Surely the earth has nothing new
        For a fugitive like me.
The past
Lives on:
Dreaming,
Buying,
Reminiscing.
People go on feasting
With funeral breaks;
Their eyes digging in their mind
For a bone to feed a new hunger.
And China's Wall still tells its story,
And the earth still has its Sisyphus
Yet the stone doesn't know what it wants.

Postman,
You've made a mistake.
        Surely nothing has changed.
Go back.
What do you want . . .

Conversation at the Bend in the Road

Haven't you slept . . . sad guard,
When do you sleep?
You haven't slept in the light of our lamp for a thousand years,
You, crucified between his outstretched palms for years,
Don't you ever sleep?
For the twentieth time . . . I want to sleep,

I fall asleep but can never sleep.
For the fiftieth time
I fell asleep but couldn't sleep
For sleep to the sad guard
Remains like the edge of a knife.
I'm afraid of sleeping
I'm afraid of waking to dreams.

Let them burn Rome . . . let them burn Berlin
Let them steal the wall of China.
You have to sleep . . .
It's time this sad guard
Had a rest for a moment . . . he sleeps
I sleep . . . and Berlin burns every second
And every hour a wall is stolen from China
And within a blink a dragon is born.
I'm afraid of sleeping
For sleep to the sad guard
Remains like the edge of a knife.

Guilty even if I were Innocent

In a room on the seventh floor
They met . . .
Talked
Made love violently
Then slept
And the curtains were drawn
In a room on the seventh floor
. . . .
But I remained pinned on the wall
And as you wished me
I remained like a nail
Seeing through their eyes
Reading their secrets
Burrowing through the wall
Of a room on the seventh floor
. . . .

Sir, I heard her
Asking him about his marvellous love
About a body –
Beg your pardon Sir –
She told him: It burns like fire
It burns me like fire
And once they talked about a vanished world
About a droplet in a vanished world
But I
And as you wished me . . . and as you created me
I couldn't understand what they said
Because I was above their marvellous love
Above the body which is like fire
And as you'd warned me: 'People are criminals'
'All people are criminals'
'Even the innocent love in their eyes'
And as you wished me
I remained like a nail
Seeing through their eyes
Reading their secrets
Burrowing through the wall
Of a room on the seventh floor
Searching in the whispers, laughter and conversation
For the moment of vengeance
For the anger of the revolutionaries
For a hope that becomes a noose round their necks
And a nail in their hands

. . . .

I beg your pardon, Sir
They were insistent in their innocence
They were insistent in their innocence

And when daylight awoke in my city
The news broadcast mentioned
The story of a room on the seventh floor
The moment of vengeance
The anger of the revolutionaries
And they had a noose round their necks and a nail
In their hands

The Dead Witness

Who killed the last commando . . . ?
I know who
I know who blinded him and who
Cut his hands and who,
Your highness, blew up
His great dream
I know who
Because I looked after that child for years
Before he was born in our dreams
                    In our longing
Before he lay in ambush at the bend in the road
Before love became his world
And the earth his dreams
Ah,
Before this young man
Became
A bleeding wound,
The blood of vengeance on the knife
I know who
I know who killed
The last commando, your highness

I know who
For a thousand, thousand nights I stayed at his door
Stayed awake in the blackness of his eyelashes
I was part of his bitter night
A glimpse of light in his exile
. . . .
And a thousand thousand times
I was the mud-spattered blood in his skin
I know who
– Who killed the last commando . . . ?
– Who killed the . . .
– I know who
– Say who
– Who's who
– If I said who

I would become, your highness,
The dead witness of the last commando

You and I, your highness,
You and I

My Apologies

My apologies, my honoured guests,
The newsreader lied in his last bulletin:
There is no sea in Baghdad
Nor pearls
Not even an island,
And everything Sinbad said
About the queens of the jinn
About the ruby and coral islands
About the thousand thousands flowing from the sultan's hand
Is a myth born in the summer heat
    Of my small town
In the burnt-up shadows of the midday sun
In the silent nights of the exiled stars.
We used to have
A sea, shells, pearls
    And a polished moon
And fishermen returning in the evening;
We used to have,
Said the newsreader's last bulletin,
An innocent, dream paradise;
For we, my honoured guests,
Lie to be born again,
Lie to stretch in our long history
The myth told by Sinbad –
We used to have
A sea, shells, pearls
    And the hour of birth.

My apologies, my honoured guests,
The newsreader lied in his last bulletin:

There is no sea in Baghdad
Nor pearls
Not even an island.

MAJALLAT SHI'R MOVEMENT

YUSUF AL-KHAL

Prayers in a Temple

1

The stone speaks. The stone becomes bread, becomes
wine, becomes. The stone is the sky, lucky is the one who
has wings.

Ah, how much I love you tonight.

For the first time I've embraced you like this. I strip naked
inside you – I am. For the first time I am the stone – the sky.

Your eyes . . . Your body is a child swimming in the
water. I love the child and the water, the water and the child.

In the wilderness nothing is friendly except the stone, in
spite of its roughness one lies on it and is comfortable.

Let this moment be for us. The stone is the sky and we are
its wings.

2

When I wake, the river wakes with me, flows and fills the
plain. I will set the sail of the day. I am alone. The friend I
was expecting has not yet arrived.

When I wake, the light is sitting in front of me. Why don't
you wake up, silly wound, take up your bed and walk away.

The walls are shrinking. The eyes of the air are fluttering.
The foot is stamping on the road. No murmur in the light.
Screaming is the secret word.

When I wake, my love wakes with me.

3

My legs are made of reeds, I will look for a crutch.

I've found it: a blond silk thread.

I will walk to the end of the earth. In the plains. On the
mountains. At night. During the day. I will walk like a
dream reached on waking.

My love is with me. My body is with me. My God is with
me. Get up, fate, and let me have your place.

4

From a distance my oak tree shades me and takes care of
me. Stretches its arms to me. It has a nest with two spar-
rows.

And here I am singing. In the courtyard there is an apple tree whose fruit gives juice for my throat.

I love my oak tree very much. Because of it I am here. Because of it I sing.

During the day I dream of the shade, and at night I embrace it and fall asleep.

I will lift the sun with my wings. I nail it, and it does not move. My oak tree's shade is my only comfort.

5

Tonight I've climbed the ivory towers. My stairs were your blue hair.

Ah, and on your altar I offered sacrifices: a pair of turtle-doves and a ewe I fattened for the sacrifice. And here I am descending to the foot of the mountain with my only child. The wounds of joy are screaming, and my days are as silent as the hand.

At dawn I will take my sheep to pasture, and in the evening I will sing for them the song of homecoming.

And now let me scream.

My body is receding, leaving me like a stranger – a rider I've never seen before.

6

Your eyes are streams of appeal. How delicious is your soft mouth. Your tongue makes the body, and your breathing gives the breath of life.

What a goddess you are! Your paradise is no temptation to sin. All its fruits are for me. I am its first man.

Embrace me, happiness. On your body I sailed my boat whose oars are lusts that never die.

Let the winds bring what they want. I am an experienced sailor, my boat is the cedar of love.

Embrace me, my little goddess. Fold your horizons around me. Love me more than love. My past is a deep fathomless wound.

7

Do not fold your dress like this. Let him enter. Let him ascend. Your breasts are peaks. Their slopes are tempting, opening to the dreams of the body.

In your garden I will plant a scion of roses.

And if I'm still alive in the autumn, I will uproot the boxthorn bushes and replace them with light and wind.

Today let us rejoice.

For some time my tongue has not tasted honey. My nails do not wound yet.

Stand naked before me and I will show you the keys of life.

Ah, let him enter!

The light of life is faint. Its presence always draws on procreation.

8

Your bedroom window is suspended on a cloud. Why do you open it and disappear?

Who will prepare the table today, unroll before me the carpet of joy, embrace my loneliness in the shade, and save my face from shame?

My existence is a wave of secrecy your strange body deciphers.

No slaves on my ships, nor slave girls, pines, fine purple clothes and jewellery of glass and stone.

Only one word and little action on my ships.

And now the city is surrendering to assault. Its walls are falling.

I am like Thammuz. My blood is a drink for the thirsty and my body is a feast for lovers.

We are all hungry for the body and thirsty for the essence of the soul.

Enough, She Said

Enough, she said.
The pain is on my lips
The pain is in my breast
I'm all in pain.
Enough.
Turn off the light and sleep,
Black spots stain the dawnlight.

I will sleep
And the world will sleep with me

No dreams
To wake us. The death of dreams awakens us.

Waking is a forest
Burning to ashes.

The Harvest

I will wait for the harvest. One more crescent moon to
come. My scythe is as fine as the body of a woman moved by
love.

I will gather the crops, one by one, and stack my granar-
ies.

Come, my friends, help yourselves.

There is hunger in our father's house. It hasn't rained for a
thousand seasons. The soil is like acne on the earth's body.

My times are mounds of emptiness.

The plants spring up again. The river reaches the sea. The
traveller returns home. The dream crosses the threshold.

Until he comes, minutes of our lives, sing, undress and
wash in your own presence, pencil your eyes with the
moment's flash.

What is coming is not born yet, our loved son is present.

One more crescent moon.

My scythe dances in the field, my granaries burst with the
season's crops.

Come, my friends, help yourselves.

And when the time comes we will sow for another season.

The Last Supper

We have bread and wine. The teacher is not with us. Our
wounds are rivers of silver.

There are deep cracks in the upper room walls. The wind
is at the window. A night traveller at the door.

We eat and drink. Our wounds are rivers of silver.

The upper room is about to collapse. The wind tears the
windows apart. And the night traveller breaks in.

Let us say: Now let us have food and drink. Our God is

dead, let us have another God. We are tired of the Word. Our souls long for the innocence of the root.

Let us say: Let the upper room crumble. The wind will pity us, the night traveller will sit with us. He is hungry for bread and thirsty for vintage wine.

Let us say: Perhaps the night traveller is our new God, the winds are fresh flowers opening to the unknown.

We go on eating and drinking, the teacher is absent. Our wounds are rivers of silver.

And when the cock crows, few will bear witness to the Lord of the earth.

Let the Roots Speak

The trees break their silence and weep over their ancient god. No leaves on the body. The roots are their only dress.

There is water in the garden.

The air floats in a vacuum. The light floats in a vacuum. Space floats in a vacuum.

And here comes the guard with his stick, on his shoulder a paper sword, in his mouth a whistle of salt roots.

Only the sparrows remain in the garden. The large birds stare at the dawn. Still they see nothing.

The garden is without a fence.

The plain is climbing the mountain. The mountain is rising to the sea. And the sea is a forest of pregnancy and birth.

The trees weep over their ancient god. He is not dead yet. His arm is a cloud in the sky of silence.

Let the roots speak. Let your tears return to the earth.

The Long Poem

I

I see no leader among the crowd. The swan strains itself on the lake. No eagles in the sky. The waters are still and the banks are nearer than one's nose. The air is heavy. The light is fierce. The donkey speaks without a miracle. The blind can see without a miracle. And the dead rise without a miracle. The miracle is a figure in a machine, but heaven remains a mystery.

I spoke in silence. The woman beside me is a tattered dress.

I will drink from an empty glass. I will smile with my lipless mouth. I will reap a field I sowed in the dark.

I am the night, and the robbers are waiting for me.

2

I will plant a bottle on the pavement and take it for a woman. A bit, a bit of warmth. My body is as cold as the curse.

I've chewed *qat* for a thousand years. I've ridden a dead horse for a thousand years. I've lived without a face for a thousand years. My mask is a tombstone.

Now I'm a balding man with forged money – a tourist without identity.

The wind plays the flute, my procession.

3

On the coast of Lebanon I stood and screamed: How long will I go on dying but never die? How long will I have to wait for the man who said: 'I will return'? How long will I have to wait for the high tide, and cry on the edge of a cliff at the low tide?

I want to die: plant me, O wind.

I want the loved one to return: pity me, O waves.

The wild bushes pray without incense. No crosses in the temple. No images on the wall. The doors are open but no one enters.

Help me, absent one.

The wolf is eating but I'm hungry. The wall jumps as I sit down. The stones are a heap of fire and lust. I am ice cubes in a glass of spirits.

Say hello, happiness. Your child is laughing on the grass. Your man is racing with the wind. And time sits like a cripple under an autumn sun.

I am a dead man. So what is there to worry about? I am immortal. Why should I be a yesman?

Kill me so I may live.

Qat: A plant whose leaves Yemenis chew at social gatherings in the afternoon.

4

Spit at my face, Master. Your throne is a toothless mouth.

5

Who is this man running on the sand, crouching on the margins of books – this blind driver?

6

I gaze at the sky, and my forehead touches gloom. The loved one left and has not returned. Since spring I've waited and cried.

Clouds. No sails in sight. High tide is empty, even of sand. Low tide is like a miser's hand. And the nets are palms nailed to the face of the wind.

There is honeycomb and colocynth in my mouth.

7

Strike me, I am a Babylonian whose gardens are suspended on street noise.

Strike me. Don't hesitate. In the upper room you kissed me twice. You had silver coins in your pocket.

Strike me. I will not sit on a stone. My neck is without roots, my body an abandoned crutch.

8

Stop dancing over my grave. I'm not dead yet. Since dawn I've looked around but could see no leader among the crowd.

The king's soldiers are rats whose weapons are feet sinking in a throne of dirt.

I am the quiet forest, says a coward; the bend in the road, says a broken chair.

My words are as dry as coal, black as a hearse.

9

This fallen fruit, humiliation. This artificial soil, destruction.

We count our fingers in front of the blind, in front of the sultan we are as silent as rugs.

Raise your hats, you unemployed.

The Trinity that frightened you has become one whose bread is stone, its wine tar for scabies.

10

To Abduna'il I tell my story. To his slaves and concubines this passing hymn.

The last days are at the door. Their hours are on finger-tips.

Defeat is a flag held high, the pains of birth are seas in flames.

Lord, give us the sign.

ADONIS

The New Noah

I

We sailed in the Ark
Our oars were God's promises.
Under the rain and dirt
We survived, but not mankind.
We went along with the waves
And the sky was like a rope of dead people
On which we tied our lives.
Through a window of prayers we reached the sky.

'Lord, why did you save us above all other
People and creatures?
Where will you throw us, to your other land,
To our original home,
To the leaves of death, to the wind of life?
Lord, our fear of the sun
Runs in our blood. We have lost faith in light,
We have lost faith in tomorrow
Where we used to begin a new life.
Oh, if only we had not been a seed
Of creation, of the earth,
If only we had remained soil or live coals,
If only we had stayed half-way
So as not to see the world,
So as not to see its hell and its God twice.'

II

If time was to start all over again
And life's face was covered with water
And the earth trembled and God was mad
And Noah asked me: 'Save the living'
I would not listen to God,
I would go about on my Ark
Clearing the pebbles and dirt

From the sockets of the dead,
Opening their souls to the flood,
Whispering in their veins:
We have returned from our wanderings,
We have come out of the cave
And changed the sky of years,
We are sailing and fear cannot bend us,
And we do not listen to God's word.

We have an appointment with death,
We have become familiar with our shores of despair,
We have grown to accept its frozen sea with iron water
And we sail through it to its end.
We carry on moving and never listen to that God,
We long for a new god.

The Wound

1

The leaves sleeping under the winds
Are boats from the wound.
The buried past is the glory of the wound.
The trees growing in your eyelashes
Are lakes for the wound.

The wound is in the crosspoint
When the grave reaches
When patience reaches
The tips of our love, our death.
The wound is a sign
The wound is in the crossing.

2

I give the voice of the wound
To a speech with choked bells.
I light the fire of the wound
For a stone coming from far away,
For a dried-up world, for drought,
For time carried on a stretcher of ice.

When history burns in my clothes
And blue nails grow in my book,
When I shout at daylight
'Who are you, who's thrown you on my books,
On my virgin land?'
I see in my books, in my virgin land
Eyes of dust.
I hear someone saying:
'I am the flourishing wound
Of your small history.'

3

I have called you a cloud,
Wound, turtle-dove of departure.
I have called you a feather and a book.
And here I am starting conversation
With a noble word
In the shifting of islands,
In the archipelago of the noble fall.
And here I am teaching conversation
To the wind and palm trees,
Wound, turtle-dove of departure.

4

If I had havens in a country of mirrors and dreams,
If I had a ship,
If I had the remains of a city,
Or a city
In a country of children and weeping

I'd have made out of all this for the wound
A song like a spear
Piercing trees, stones and heaven,
And soft as water,
Overpowering and thrilling like a conquest.

5

Rain on our deserts,
World charged with a dream and longing.
Rain and shake us, we the palm trees of the wound,
And snap two branches for us
From the trees that love the silence of the wound,
From the trees that stay awake over the wound
With arched eyelashes and hands.

World charged with a dream and longing,
World falling on my forehead
And drawn like a wound,
Don't come closer, the wound is nearer than you,
Don't tempt me, the wound is more beautiful than you.
The wound is beyond the fate
Your eyes cast
On the lost civilizations.
It's left no sails
Nor islands.

The Fire Tree

A family of crinkled leaves
Fell by a spring.
They hurt the land of tears,
They read the book of fire
To the water.

My family didn't wait for me.
They left
No fire, no marks.

A Mirror for the Twentieth Century

A coffin bearing the face of a boy
A book

Written on the belly of a crow
A wild beast hidden in a flower

A rock
Breathing with the lungs of a lunatic:

This is it
This is the Twentieth Century.

A Mirror for Autumn

Have you seen a woman
Carrying the corpse of Autumn?
Have you seen a woman
Rubbing her face on the pavement,
Weaving a dress
With threads of rain?
People
Are burnt-out coals
On the pavement.

The Minaret

A stranger arrived.
The minaret wept:
He bought it and topped it with a chimney.

Invasion

The birds are burning,
The horses, the women and the pavements:
Breadcrumbs in Tamerlane's hands.

The Bird

On mount Sinnin
I heard a bird
Crying for peace.

Its songs
Cut through
The city's coldness
Like razor blades.

The Desert

The Diary of Beirut under Siege, 1982

I

1
The cities break up
The land is a train of dust
Only poetry knows how to marry this space.

2
No road to his house – the siege.
And the streets are graveyards;
          Far away a stunned moon
          Hangs on threads of dust
          Over his house.

3
I said: This street leads to our house. He said: No.
          You won't pass. And pointed his bullets at me.

Fine, in every street
          I have homes and friends.

4
Roads of blood,
          The blood a boy was talking about
          And whispering to his friends:

Only some holes known as stars
Remain in the sky.

5
The voice of the city is soft
The face of the city glows
Like a little boy telling his dreams to the night
And offering his chair to the morning.

6
They found people in sacks:
    One without a head
    One without a tongue or hands
    One strangled
    The rest without shape or names.
Have you gone mad? Please,
                       Don't write about these things.

7
In a page of a book
Bombs see themselves,
Prophetic sayings and ancient wisdom see themselves,
Niches see themselves.
The thread of carpet words
Go through memory's needle
Over the city's face.

8
The killer
In the air
Swims in the city's wound –
             The wound is the fall
             That shakes with its name,
             With its bleeding name
Everything around us.
The houses leave their walls
And I am not I

9

There may come a time when you'll be
Accepted to live deaf and dumb, and perhaps
They'll let you mumble: death,
                    Life, resurrection –
                    And peace be upon you.

10

From the palm wine to the calmness of the desert . . . etc.
From the morning that smuggles its stomach and sleeps on the corpses
    of the refugees . . . etc.
From the streets, army vehicles, concentration of troops . . . etc.
From the shadows, men, women . . . etc.
From the bombs stuffed with the prayers of Muslims and infidels . . .
    etc.
From the flesh of iron that bleeds and sweats pus . . . etc.
From the fields that long for the wheat, the green and the workers . . .
    etc.
From the castles walling our bodies and bombarding us with darkness
    . . . etc.
From the myths of the dead which speak of life, express life . . . etc.
From the speech which is the slaughter, the slaughtered and the
    slaughterers . . . etc.
From the dark dark dark
I breathe, feel my body, search for you and him, myself and others,
And hang my death
Between my face and these bleeding words . . . etc.

11

You will see
    Say his name
    Say I painted his face
    Stretch your hands to him
    Or smile
    Or say I was once sad
    Or say I was once happy
You will see
    There is no homeland . . .

12

The killing has changed the city's shape – This rock
        Is a boy's head
        This smoke people breathing.

13

Everything sings of his exile/a sea
                        Of blood – what
Do you expect from these mornings other than their veins sailing
In the mists, on the waves of the massacre?

14

Keep her company at night, stay longer with her at night,
She's placed death on her lap,
And turned over her days
                Like old papers.
Keep the last pictures
       Of her landscape.
She's turning in her own sand,
In a pool of sparks,
And on her body
She has scars of people crying.

15

Seeds are scattered in our land,
So keep the secret of this blood,
Fields that nourish our myths –
       I'm talking about the zest of the seasons
       About the lightning in space.

16

Bourje Square – (inscriptions whispering their secrets
              to broken bridges . . .)
Bourje Square – (memory looking for itself)
              in fire and dust . . .)
Bourje Square – (an open desert
            swept and dragged by the winds . . .)

Bourje Square – (witchcraft
                 to see corpses moving / their limbs
                 in a backstreet / their ghosts
                 in a backstreet / you hear them sighing . . .)
Bourje Square – (west and east)
                 gallows standing,
                 martyrs and guardians . . .)
Bourje Square – (a trail
                 of caravans: myrrh
                       frankincense and musk
                 and spices opening the festival . . .)
Bourje Square – (a trail
                 of caravans: thunder
                       and explosion and lightning
                 and hurricanes opening the festival . . .)
Bourje Square – (I have called this era
                       by the name of this place)

17
– Corpses or rubble,
Beirut's face?
– Bells ringing or people screaming?
– A friend?
– You? Hello.
Have you been away? Just back? What's new?
– They killed a neighbour . . . /
. . . .
       playing games /
– Your dice is stronger today,
– Luck /

        . . . .
        Dark
        And words dragging words

II

1
My era tells me bluntly:
You do not belong.

I answer bluntly:
I do not belong,
I try to understand you.
Now I am a shadow
Lost in the desert
And shelter in the tent of a skull.

2

The distance shrinks, a window recedes.
Daylight is a thread
Snipped by my lungs to stitch the evening.

3

All I said about my life and death
Recurs in the silence
Of the stone under my head . . .

4

Am I full of contradictions? That is correct.
　　Now I am a plant. Yesterday, when I was between fire and water,
　　I was a harvest.
　　Now I am a rose and live coal,
　　Now I am the sun and the shadow
　　I am not a god.
Am I full of contradictions? That is correct.

5

The door of my house is closed.
Darkness is a blanket:
　　A pale moon comes with
　　A handful of light
　　My words fail
　　To convey my gratitude.

6

He shuts the door
Not to trap his joy
. . . But to free his grief.

7
Whatever comes will be old
   So take with you anything other than this madness – get ready
                           To stay a stranger.

8
The sun no longer rises
It covers its feet with straw
And slips away . . .

9
I expect death to come at night
   To cushion his lap with
                           A rose
Tired of the dust covering the forehead of dawn
Tired of the breathing of people.

10
The night descends (these are the papers he gave to the ink – morning's
   ink that never came)
The night descends on the bed (the bed of the lover who never came)
The night descends/not a sound (clouds. Smoke)
The night descends (someone has in his hands rabbits? Ants?)
The night descends (the wall of the building shakes. All the curtains are
   transparent)
The night descends, listens (the stars as the night knows are dumb, and
   the last trees at the end of the wall remember nothing of what the air
   said to their branches)
The night descends (the wind whispers to the windows)
The night descends (the light penetrates. A neighbour lies in his
   nakedness)
The night descends (two people. A dress holding a dress – and the
   windows are transparent)
The night descends (this is a whim: the moon complains to its trousers
   about what the lovers have always complained of)
The night descends (he relaxes in a pitcher filled with wine. No friends
   just one man turning in his glass)
The night descends (carries a few spiders, feels at ease with insects
   which are a pest only to houses/signs of light: an angel coming,

missiles or invitations? Our women neighbours have gone on
  pilgrimage/come back less slim and more coquettish)
The night descends (he enters between the breasts of the days/our
  women neighbours are my days)
The night descends (that sofa/that pillow: this is an alleyway, this is a
  place)
The night descends (what shall we prepare? Wine? Meat, soup and
  bread? The night hides from us its appetite)
The night descends (he plays for a short while with his snails, with
  strange doves which came from an unknown land, and with the
  insects not mentioned in the chapters of the book about reproduction
  among different animal species)
The night descends (thunder – or is it the noise of angels coming on
  their horses?)
The night descends (he mumbles, turning in his glass . . .)

11
Who would show me a planet
  To give me ink to write about my night?

12
He wrote a poem
        (how can I convince him my future is a desert?)
He wrote a poem
        (who will shake the stoneness of words off me?)
He wrote a poem
        (you don't belong if you don't kill a brother)
He wrote a poem
        (how can we understand this fugitive language caught
        between the question and the poem?)
He wrote a poem
        (can the refugee dawn embrace its sun?)
He wrote a poem
        (there's confusion between the sun's face and the sky)
He wrote a poem (. . ./let him die . . .)

13
Should I talk? On what?
        In what direction?
I ask you, seagull flying in the blueness of the sea . . .

Who said I asked, who said
I'm gazing at the sea or talking to the seagull?

I never was
I never walked
I never said . . .

14

I'll contradict myself.
I'll add to my dictionary:
I don't belong to my language, my mouth
Not once was it my mouth.
Ah, star of destruction, blood rose.

15

I should have been torn to pieces, thrown in a forest fire
To light the road.
Friend,
Tiredness,
Give me your kind hand
Give me what your nights took from my bleeding sun.

16

Anything rejected by other eyes will be looked after by my eyes.
This is my friendship's promise to destruction.

17

Since I surrendered myself to myself and asked
What is the difference between destruction and myself,
I have lived the poet's optimum life:
No answer.

18

After poetry had torn time's dress
I called on the winds
To stitch the rags to the place.

19

What is it that touched Mutanabbi
     Other than this soil that felt his tread?
He betrayed many things,
But not his vision.

20

You do not die because you are created
     Or because you have a body
You die because you are the face of the future.

21

Let
My dream neglect my body
And my body betray its floating sleeplessness.

22

I should call a wolf to shine the mirror of the sheep
     That forgot their own image.

23

We no longer meet,
Rejection and exile keep us apart.
The promises are dead, space is dead,
Death alone
Has become our meeting point.

24

The flower
     That tempted the wind to carry its perfume
Died yesterday.

25

My tiredness sleeps like a bird, but I remain
     Like a branch.
I'll say nothing now, I won't disturb its sleep.

26

The cover is torn, and the translator unmasked
By the fire wearing the face of the place.

27

A cafe – the sea sleeps like a child/
I know this face. 'Hello, how are you?'
I know this voice . . .
'The fortune teller hasn't come today . . .'
'Is he ill? Has he left?'
     'Strangers dropped him
     In a well . . .'
. . ./the sea sleeps like a child.

28

A bat
  Claims the light is dark,
  And the sun a road to the grave,
Then babbles on.
        The bat didn't fall,
Only the child asleep in dawn's lap fell off.

29

You're not this city or that city
  You're not the sojourn and the memories/the borders are your
    hostages – your steps are frightened.
The histories of the sky you were
  Are shadows,
  Sparks of a dying flame.

30

A creator devoured by his creatures, a country
  Hiding in the blood running from his remains.
This is the beginning of a new era.

31

Whenever I say: my country is within reach
    And bears fruit in a reachable language
Another language kicks me
To another language.

32

Trees bow to say goodbye
Flowers open, glow, lower their leaves to say goodbye,
Roads like pauses between the breathing and the words say goodbye,
A body wears sand, falls in a wilderness to say goodbye,
The papers that love ink,
                    The alphabet, the poets say goodbye,
And the poem says goodbye.

33

All the certainty I have lived slips away
All the torches of my desire slip away
All that was between the faces that lit my exile and me slips away
I have to start from the beginning
To teach my limbs to reach the future,
To talk, to climb, to descend from the beginning
In the sky of beginnings, in the abyss of the alphabet.

34

They are falling, the land is a thread of smoke
                    Time a train
                    Travelling along a track of smoke . . .
My obsession is here now, loss.
My concern is the end
                    Is not over.
They are falling, I am not looking for a new beginning.

UNSI AL-HAJ

Memory

This
Long
Night!

The ostriches are burying me

The Days and the Giants

I love the memory of the days that walked walked and
never knew they'd end up in a book. I love working hours
wrapped in mist and the giants who walked walked and
never knew they'd end up in a book.

I love the memory of the days that will come, these
present days.

Girl Butterfly Girl

A girl dreamt she was a butterfly
      She got up
And didn't know whether she was
A girl dreaming she was a butterfly
Or
A butterfly dreaming it was a girl

After hundreds of years
The air at night
My children,
Was a boy and girl frolicking like a butterfly
Who dreamt it was a boy and a girl
          Or
A boy and a girl dreaming they were a butterfly

The wind grew strong
A butterfly
My children,
Fell to pieces outside

SHAUQI ABI SHAQRA

The Storm

We must sleep like air
Dream of rebellion
The holiday on this earth is finished
And heaven's suitcases are packed
We must pray
For the young father
Prepare supper
We must buy a storm
From the representative of winter

Children of a Grieved Mother

This is our mother.
Her eyes are always on us
And sometimes she's forgiving.

Come on children.
We get on her lap.
We're not rich
Her glances are our only bread
Her loneliness is our only roof.

Come on children.
On the day of the Cross we set the poems on fire.
At supper time we set the war on fire without matches.

Returning to Granny

Granny
The children will return
Like boats
Will go round your crumbled hut

Will catch the moon
So you can see visitors' shoes
So your heart's longing
Can blow proverbs in our faces
Like a country fox
So we can grow and climb the world like trees

The Hotel

Here every soldier
Flings his helmet from the mountain top
And sees
Men drinking *araq*
In our hotel

We are a friendly people
We don't start wars
We don't block roads
Like other people

Here we are like gloves in the rain
Opening a hotel to the Magi
To the eyes of the prophets
Like a photo album

The Prison's Stream

With table wines
And pitchers of hope
I kneel down to wash
The prisoners' clothes in my cage

As I start I call my guard
And spit out poems
In all directions

Araq: Anisette.

And throw my innocent dreams
At his feet

I am the prison's helpless stream
And my life is as cold
As the caliph's dinars

Miss Lemonada

Miss Lemonada is running outside the garden. She hates goblets.

She's a country tent. Skiers, philatelists and sex-maniacs flock to her.

Villages and hills breathe through her body. She stands like a ring. When she laughs I can do without a bunch of jasmines. When she weeps the steel workers adore her and the world stops going to work.

She sleeps on a silk pillow. The poor see her nose as white as flour.

If war breaks out we'll wear balloons and disappear in the air. A partridge passes by and we eat it.

On a straw boat she sails through rocks. A shepherd and his brave sons applaud her.

I leave her alone and sleep on the roof. I hear the call of her flesh. I keep away from her long nails. I walk her to the church and bathe her in strong light.

A peacock feather fan. Wanders in the valley. A peasant woman wears the folklore.

The Fan and the Observatory Dome

The world, as fine as a razor-blade, cuts my chin. The police chase me like fish.

I play, making a paper star. The Magi follow its light. An Ethiopian servant holds my fan.

I fly on a straw towards the windows and put out the honeymoon lantern.

I climb the rays of the teeth. Incense rises from me. I carve an angel to be eaten on the road like a raisin.

I sit like a ball outside the playground eating snow. I travel on a reed. I carry coloured eggs, fledgelings and oil.

Wearing shorts, like a notebook, I jump from the observatory dome to the planets. I open my shirt and breathe air.

I have made a lion from a stone. The gnats and the secrets of the small world will fall on it.

Fresh Air

I jump on one leg for joy. All the families invite me to give them children and horses to take them over the wind.

I milk a nannygoat and keep it going on school uniforms and stage curtains. I grab it by the horns and it starts up like a car and comes full butt upon dogs and actors.

No thorns in the clouds.

I teach the flock to ride bicycles to outrace the wolves and the aristocratic lady.

My cousin is a shepherd girl in a museum. My sister skis and scoops up snow and sports. Her son is a plant. My mother is a rock on which I cross the river.

I read stars, hair-styles, gramarye, and meet scientists and peasants. I open the cellar for my donkey. It's an inventive beast which kicks at the moon, bites travellers, raises its ears above my head and rolls itself in olive oil and storms. The donkey is made of wax and steel. I set it alight to brighten the world at the eclipse of the sun.

I reduce the hotel to a flower and expose its sheets and its underwear.

I draw a lantern. I write a story of a girl who falls under the Cross, a butterfly sucks her gland.

Hens, pigeons and a small flag showing the colours of an embassy hover above my forehead.

I don't wear trousers nor a waistcoat nor a tarboosh, because I'm not the village headman.

On Good Friday I congeal before the Cross and become soap.

Summer. The cold returns home to the pole like an eagle. A miracle happens. My nannygoat starts off with a bucket of milk and takes the pictures and the pens with it.

The Silver Mouth

I always crane my neck to see more of the giraffe.

A poem: a white hair on a widow's head.

We dive in the sea. We swim to the great beam. We shake hands with the captain. The immigration officer stamps our backs: You are the journey.

In a café we drink whisky and scratch our heads.

I wait for a wild boar to pop out his brains like roses from a window.

A poet's poverty is long nails. One day he pares them with a pair of scissors.

Angelica is an American. Accompanied by a nurse and a dog. Once she was fatally bitten by a serpent. The nurse followed the dog but didn't see the serpent slithering into the desert.

The Shauf mountain – that clean shepherd who plays Mijanu and Abu al-Zuluf music.

That orchard of emirs and shaikhs – swells the belly of a peasant with figs and wheat, grows medlars, acorn and oak trees whose odour the passengers smell as the bus swings into view.

My Arms Became the Month of October

Sunday ran away from a priest like a nannygoat. I was quick in catching it and the bell rang rang rang. When my love arrived and the Holy Mass burst into light, my arms became the month of October, my sweat was kept in a baptismal font and the sky was a bird and a string.

Shauf mountain: The home of the Lebanese Druze emirs and famous for its cedar groves.
Mijanu and Abu al-Zuluf music: Different kinds of Levantine folk songs.

FU'AD RIFQA

Setting Off

Don't ask from where you came
Let my hands
Dream
Of a voyage
Into languages, strange islands.
I've become the poem of return,
A return to foreign springs.

Don't ask from where you came
Let my hands dream for a while.

An Elegy for Hölderlin

It is you.
We know from the cries in the wind
The clouds are bringing the church's psalms.

The door is closed.
Fertility's priestesses have slipped out
Of the incense burners to the funerals
Leaving the agony of the church
In the braziers standing in cold corners.

Straw Mat

I remember we had a straw mat
Which liked me
And used to tell me:
The feast is coming tomorrow, my child,
And the church will be
Full of laurels and candles.

The feast arrived, followed by other feasts,
And I wore them like a dress.
At the rituals I carried
An incense burner whose heaven was Jesus.

All at once the smoke
Changed its course,
And moved away from the Christmas bell,
And did not return
As the host for the stones of the church.

In my village
We had a straw mat
As old as time.

MUHAMMAD AL-MAGHUT

The Noonday Sun and the Shade

All the fields of the world
Are at odds with two small lips
All the streets of history
Are at odds with two bare feet.

They travel
We stay
They own the gallows
We own the necks
They own the pearls
We own the warts and freckles
They own night, dawn, afternoon and daylight
And we own the skin and bones.

We plant in the heat of the noonday sun
They eat in the shade
Their teeth are as white as rice
Ours as black as a jungle
Their chests are soft as silk
Ours as drab as execution squares.
Yet we are the kings of the world.
Their homes are stacked with classified files
Ours with autumn leaves.
In their pockets they keep the addresses of thieves and traitors
In our rivers and thunder.

They own the windows
We own the winds
They own the ships
We own the waves
They own the medals
We own the dirt
They own the walls and balconies

We own the scarves and daggers.
But now we must sleep on the pavement, my love.

The Postman's Fear

Prisoners everywhere
Send me all you have
Fears screams and boredom
Fishermen of all beaches
Send me all you have
Empty nets and seasickness

Peasants of every land
Send me all you have
Flowers rags
Mutilated breasts
Ripped-up bellies
And torn-out nails
To my address. . . any café
Any street in the world
I'm preparing a *huge file*
About human suffering
To present to God
Once it's signed by the lips of the hungry
And the eyelids of those still waiting
You wretched everywhere
What I fear most is
God could be *illiterate*

Siege

My tears are blue
From gazing at the sky – I wept for so long
My tears are yellow
From dreaming of golden ears of corn –
I wept so much

Let the generals go to wars
Lovers to the forests
Scientists to the labs
I'll look for a rosary and an old chair
And become the man I used to be
The caretaker at sorrow's threshold
Since all the resters and religions
Confirm I'll die
Hungry or in prison

Tourist

My childhood is far away . . . my old age is far away . . .
My country is far away . . . my exile is far away . . .
Tourist,
Can I borrow your binoculars
I might see a hand
Or a handkerchief waving to me in this world.
Take a picture of me in rags,
Squatting and crying in front of a hotel;
And scribble on the back of the photo:
An Arab poet.

Spread your white handkerchief on the pavement
And sit beside me under this gentle rain,
And I'll tell you a secret:
Tell your guides to go,
Throw your notes and impressions
In the dustbin . . . in the fire,
Because any old peasant
Can sing you the history of the Arabs
In a ballad
As he rolls a cigarette by his tent.

Winter

Like wolves in periods of drought
We grew everywhere
We loved the rain
We loved the autumn
One day we even thought
Of sending a letter of thanks to the sky
With an autumn leaf as a postage stamp
We used to believe the mountains would vanish
The seas would vanish
Civilizations would vanish
Only love was eternal
Suddenly we parted
She liked long sofas
I liked long ships
She liked to whisper and sigh in the cafés
I liked to jump and scream in the streets
And in spite of all
My arms wide as the universe
Are waiting for her . . .

An Arab Traveller in a Space Station

Scientists and technicians,
Give me a ticket to the sky:
I come on behalf of my grieved country,
Her aged, her widows, her children.
Give me a ticket to the sky
I have no money . . . only *tears*.

No place for me?
Let me stay in the hold
Or on the deck.
I'm a peasant, I'm used to it.
I won't hurt a star
I won't be rude to a cloud.
All I want is to reach

88

The sky as soon as I can
To put the whip in God's hand:
He may stir us to revolution.

The Orphan

Oh
The dream . . .
The dream . . .
My solid-gold car crashed,
The wheels scattered about like gypsies.
One spring night I had a dream
And when I woke
There were flowers on my pillow.
Once I dreamt of the sea
And in the morning
Fins and shells covered my bed.
But when I dreamt of freedom
Swords were pointed at my neck
Like a morning halo.
. . . from now on
You won't find me
At ports or on trains
But in public libraries
Sleeping on maps of Europe
Where my mouth touches rivers
And my tears run across continents.

JABRA IBRAHIM JABRA

After Golgotha

I have lived with Christ
I have died and risen with him,
My voice boomed in the open
As if it were not my own,
Feeding a fire I never started.
Why the fire? And for whom?
Give me a shadow and cold water
So I can hang my memory
On the wall of an abandoned room.

The guests and the crowd dispersed,
And the voice cried hopelessly
Like a death–rattle on Golgotha.

A taste of honey and colocynth
On my lips.

Have I returned from the dead to hear my voice
Luring me to the emptiness I escaped?
Give me a shadow.
Woman, put some ice in your water.
The sun is burning,
And life after death is a burden.
My voice loves fire.
For whom? For whom?
I closed my eyes,
A taste of honey and colocynth
On my lips.

TAUFIQ SAYIGH

What's Next

He turns comedy into tragedy,
Drops grandeur from the tragedy
And quacks:
What's next?

My world is empty.
Houses packed with
What's next.
If one day he retreats
And the world's cheeks come to life
Flashes of fear dull their colour
And thunder coughs:
What's next?

My summers are empty,
My winters a nightmare,
My life a whistling train
Passing through them.
What's next?

Morning coffee
What's next?
At work
What's next?
Facing note-papers
Or in bed
What's next?
It's the same here or there
What's next?

He chews daylight
What's next?
Leaves no traces of it for tomorrow
And cherishes yesterday's ruins

Of homes and gardens;
And hadn't been for
What's next . . .

In
What's next
I've burnt my days.

RIAD AL-RAYYES

To Taufiq Sayigh

Under the rain
I looked in my pockets
As you used to do
For my identity card
But I didn't care if I'd lost it
Because I had a country.

Under the sun
I look in my pockets
For my work permit
Because like you
I've lost my country.

ISAM MAHFOUZ

The End

My story's end
Is as cold
As leftovers
On a table.

HUZAIRAN EXPERIENCE

NIZAR QABBANI

Footnotes to the Book of the Setback

1

Friends,
The ancient word is dead.
The ancient books are dead.
Our speech with holes like worn-out shoes is dead.
Dead is the mind that led to defeat.

2

Our poems have gone sour.
Women's hair, nights, curtains and sofas
Have gone sour.
Everything has gone sour.

3

My grieved country,
In a flash
You changed me from a poet who wrote love poems
To a poet who writes with a knife.

4

What we feel is beyond words:
We should be ashamed of our poems.

5

Stirred
By Oriental bombast,
By Antaric swaggering that never killed a fly,
By the fiddle and the drum,
We went to war
And lost.

Antaric: Antar (525–615), a pre-Islamic poet and hero of a popular epic bearing his name, is the symbol of the unbeaten knight.

6

Our shouting is louder than our actions,
Our swords are taller than us,
This is our tragedy.

7

In short
We wear the cape of civilization
But our souls live in the stone age.

8

You don't win a war
With a reed and a flute.

9

Our impatience
Cost us fifty thousand new tents.

10

Don't curse heaven
If it abandons you,
Don't curse circumstances.
God gives victory to whom He wishes.
God is not a blacksmith to beat swords.

11

It's painful to listen to the news in the morning.
It's painful to listen to the barking of dogs.

12

Our enemies did not cross our borders
They crept through our weaknesses like ants.

13

Five thousand years
Growing beards
In our caves.
Our currency is unknown,
Our eyes are a haven for flies.
Friends,

Smash the doors,
Wash your brains,
Wash your clothes.
Friends,
Read a book,
Write a book,
Grow words, pomegranates and grapes,
Sail to the country of fog and snow.
Nobody knows you exist in caves.
People take you for a breed of mongrels.

14

We are a thick-skinned people
With empty souls.
We spend our days practising witchcraft,
Playing chess and sleeping.
Are we the 'Nation by which God blessed mankind'?

15

Our desert oil could have become
Daggers of flame and fire.
We're a disgrace to our noble ancestors:
We let our oil flow through the toes of whores.

16

We run wildly through the streets
Dragging people with ropes,
Smashing windows and locks.
We praise like frogs,
Swear like frogs,
Turn midgets into heroes,
And heroes into scum:
We never stop and think.
In mosques
We crouch idly,
Write poems,
Proverbs
And beg God for victory
Over our enemy.

17

If I knew I'd come to no harm,
And could see the Sultan,
I'd tell him:
'Sultan,
Your wild dogs have torn my clothes
Your spies hound me
Their eyes hound me
Their noses hound me
Their feet hound me
They hound me like Fate
Interrogate my wife
And take down the names of my friends.
Sultan,
When I came close to your walls
And talked about my pains,
Your soldiers beat me with their boots,
Forced me to eat my shoes.
Sultan,
You lost two wars.
Sultan,
Half of our people are without tongues,
What's the use of a people without tongues?
Half of our people
Are trapped like ants and rats
Between walls.'
If I knew I'd come to no harm
I'd tell him:
'You lost two wars
You lost touch with children.'

18

If we hadn't buried our unity
If we hadn't ripped its young body with bayonets
If it had stayed in our eyes
The dogs wouldn't have savaged our flesh.

19

We want an angry generation
To plough the sky
To blow up history
To blow up our thoughts.
We want a new generation
That does not forgive mistakes
That does not bend.
We want a generation
Of giants.

20

Arab children,
Corn ears of the future,
You will break our chains.
Kill the opium in our heads,
Kill the illusions.
Arab children,
Don't read about our windowless generation,
We are a hopeless case.
We are as worthless as water-melon rind.
Don't read about us,
Don't ape us,
Don't accept us,
Don't accept our ideas,
We are a nation of crooks and jugglers.
Arab children,
Spring rain,
Corn ears of the future,
You are the generation
That will overcome defeat.

I am the Train of Sadness

I travel on thousands of trains
I saddle my despair
I mount the clouds of my cigarette
In my suitcase

I keep the addresses of my lovers
Who were my lovers yesterday?

The train's travelling
Faster faster
Chewing the flesh of distances on its way
Ravaging the fields on its way
Gulping the trees on its way
Licking the feet of the lakes

The inspector asks for my ticket
And my destination
Is there a destination?
No hotel on earth knows me
Nor the addresses of my lovers

I am the train of sadness
There are no platforms
Where I could stop
In all my journeys
My platforms slip away
My stations
Slip away from me

Morphine

The word is a bouncing ball
The ruler throws from his balcony.
The people run after the ball,
Their tongues hanging out like hungry dogs.

The word in the Arab World
Is a nifty marionette
Who speaks seven languages
And wears a red cap.
He sells paradise and gaudy bangles,

Seven languages: A reference to the seven different ways of reading the Qur'an.

Sells wide-eyed children
White rabbits and doves.

The word is an overworked whore:
The writer has slept with her,
The journalist has slept with her,
The imam of the mosque has slept with her.

Since the seventh century
The word has been a shot of morphine.
Rulers calm their people with speeches.
The word in my country is a woman
Who's solicited men
Since the Book became law.

The Ruler and the Sparrow

I travelled in the Arab homeland
To read my poems.
I was convinced
Poetry was the public's bread.
I was convinced
The words were fish
And the public their water.

I travelled in the Arab homeland
With only a notebook.
Police stations tossed me about,
Soldiers tossed me about,
And all I had was a sparrow in my pocket
But the officer asked
For the sparrow's passport.
The word in my country needs a passport.

I waited for the pass
Staring at sandbags,
Reading the posters
That spoke of *one homeland*,

That spoke of *one people*.
I was discarded at my country's gates
Like broken glass.

FADWA TUQAN

To Christ

But those husbandmen said among themselves, this is the heir; come let us kill him, and the inheritance shall be ours.
And they took him, killed him, and cast him out of the vineyard.

Mark 12: 7–8

Lord, Glory of the Universe,
On Christmas Day 1967
Jerusalem's feasts were nailed upon the Cross.
Lord, on the day of your feast
The bells were silent.

For two thousand years
The bells always rang
On the day of your birth
But not this year.

Under the weight of the Cross
On the road of agony
Jerusalem is whipped:
The soldier's lashes draw blood.
But the world's heart is closed to the tragedy.
This stone–cold world, Lord, is
Blind
For the eye of the sun has turned to glass.

Not a candle was lit,
Not a tear was shed
To wash away Jerusalem's grief.

Lord, the vineworkers killed the heir
And took the vines;
The bird of sin
Feathered the sinners of the world
And swooped down to stain Jerusalem's chastity.

Lord, Glory of Jerusalem,
From the well of grief
From the abyss
                    From the depth of the night
From the heart of pain
To you Jerusalem's groans rise.
Mercy, O Lord,
Let this cup pass from her.

SAMIH AL-QASIM

Sons of War

On his wedding night
They took him to war.

Five years of hardship.

One day he returned
On a red stretcher
And his three sons
Met him at the port.

The Clock on the Wall

My city collapsed
The clock was still on the wall
Our neighbourhood collapsed
The clock was still on the wall
The street collapsed
The clock was still on the wall
The square collapsed
The clock was still on the wall
My house collapsed
The clock was still on the wall
The wall collapsed
The clock
Ticked on

The Will of a Man Dying in Exile

Light the fire so I can see in the mirror of the flames
The courtyard, the bridge
And the golden meadows.
Light the fire so I can see my tears

On the night of the massacre,
So I can see your sister's corpse
Whose heart is a bird ripped up by foreign tongues,
By foreign winds.
Light the fire so I can see your sister's corpse,
So I can see jasmine
As a shroud,
The moon
As an incense burner
On the night of the massacre.
Light the fire so I can see myself dying.
My suffering is your only inheritance,
My suffering before the jasmine turns
Into a witness.
The moon
Into a witness
Light the fire so you can see
Light the fi . . .

The Story of the Unknown Man

At the end of the road,
At the end of the road he stood
Like a scarecrow in a vineyard.
At the end of the road he stood
Like the man in the green traffic light.
At the end of the road he stood
Wearing an old coat:
His name was the 'Unknown man',
The white houses
Slammed their doors on him,
Only jasmine plants
Loved his face with its shadows of love and hate.

His name was the 'Unknown man'.
The country was
Under the weight of locusts and grief.

One day
His voice rang in the square of white houses.
Men, women and children
Thronged to the square of white houses
And saw him burning
His old coat.
(And he had an old coat.)

The sky swelled with a green cloud,
With a white cloud,
With a black cloud,
With a red cloud,
With a strange colourless cloud.

And on that day
The sky flashed and thundered,
The rain poured down
The rain poured down.
His name was the Unknown man,
Only jasmine plants
Loved his face with its shadows of love and hate
And the white houses loved him.

The General's Property

To Ariel Sharon

A flower vase on the general's table
Five roses in the vase
The general's tank has five mouths
Under the tank a boy of five, a rose
A boy and five stars adorn the general's shoulder
In his vase five boys and a rose
Under his tank five roses and five boys
The tank has countless mouths

The Boring Orbit

My daughter who's not yet born and whose name is *Hagar*
asked me: 'Daddy, why does the earth go round?'
'Early one morning God woke up
And the angel Gabriel brought Him His morning coffee.
"One sugar, please."
God stirred the sugar with his gold spoon
In dull, empty circles,
Dull circles,
Dull, empty circles.
And since that time, my child,
The earth's been rotating in its boring orbit.'

RASHID HUSSEIN

Lessons in Parsing

The First Lesson

He was sixty . . .
Still teaching.
Once he came into the class and said:
    'Parse: "The teacher came."'
    We thought he was joking
    So we laughed and answered:
        '"came"   : verb
        "teacher"   : . . . ?'
    Suddenly we understood . . . in a flash
        We fell silent,
    And heard him muttering:
        '"came"   : verb
        "teacher"   :
        He didn't come!
        The police brought him . . . but he will teach.'

The Second Lesson

We grew up together until
He was nearly seventy but
Still teaching.
For example the teacher said:
    '"My master dreams of the revolution but won't fight"
    A sentence complete in itself – a thousand times.
    Parse that and you'll become a fighter!'
    We were silent.
    We said nothing but
    Our silence in itself was fighting
                        Our silence was . . . but:
    In the class there was a boy who nourished the earth with his
       hands
    Its olives ran over his mouth.

His name was Adnan . . . a peasant with no land but
He was not silent . . . no, he was every inch a fighter.

That day he disregarded the rules of grammar
     And went on teaching:
       '"My master" : is not a subject
       "dreams"   : is not a verb
       "of"   : governed by a preposition
       "revolution"   : is not governed by a preposition
                      "but won't fight" : that is correct.'

The Lesson before the Last

A day later the teacher came into the class
As cheerful and as lively as the zest of an orange.
Although seventy, still a child . . . he greeted us and said:
'"They put Adnan in prison."
Parse that, girls,
Parse that, boys.'
We were thrilled . . . we wept . . . and we cried out:
       '"Adnan" : subject
             "prison" : object.'
We set grammar and its rules on fire
         And became fighters.

MU'IN BESSEISSO

Traffic Lights

Red light
Stop
Green light
Go
Red light
Green light
Red light
Green light
Stop
Stop
Go
Go
Red light
Red light
Where's the green light
A pregnant woman in a car
Gives birth in a car
The boy grows up
Falls in love
And gets married in a car
Has children
And reads magazines and newspapers
In a car
They round him up
And put him in the boot of a car
They draft him and he dies a martyr
Behind the windscreen of a car
They bury him under the wheels of a car
And the car is still in the street
Waiting for the green light
Red light
Stop
Green light
Go
Red light green light

To Rimbaud

When Rimbaud became a slave-trader
And threw his net
Over Ethiopia
To catch black lions
Black swans
He abandoned poetry . . .
How honest was that little boy . . .
But many poets
Became slave-traders,
Usurers,
And did not abandon poetry;
Representatives of publicity agencies
Dealers in faked paintings
And did not abandon poetry.
In the sultan's palace their poems were turned into
Doors and windows
Tables and carpets
And they did not abandon poetry . . .
They praised,
Received medals and titles,
Gold, silver and stone cups
And they did not abandon poetry . . .
The gendarme's stamp,
The gendarme's footmark on their poems
And they did not abandon poetry . . .
How honest was Rimbaud . . .
How honest was that little boy . . .

SALAH NIAZI

from *The Thinker*

Within my bolted infernal gates
I'm still alive,
Pinned on the gallery's smooth wall.
Scanning eyes
Sting my sleep.
The police
And security guards
Mine my streets, my map's gardens.
I am my own prison, my own gateless walls.

My insurance policy
Doesn't sense what I'm made of,
Doesn't sense I could be
A figure in a painting.
I wake from sleeplessness . . . the same form,
The same poise.
In sleeplessness I dream:
If I could be someone else . . . something's moving like a toy
In my mirror.
If I could be . . . nothing at all grows in my mirror.
I'm trapped within walls of thumping feet and scanning eyes.
Invisible cap,
Wadis and labyrinths scar my mind.
How can I escape
From my metallic flesh, my spattered blood,
My steel background,
And heavenly call?
My padlocks rust on my lips,
Drought whips my history.
My landscape, my schoolyards, my towns
Float in pollution and lose their breath.
My villages fight with chunks of monument.
My strained muscles, how can I pick up the pieces?

In my concrete background,
The scientific definitions
Are the size of coffins.
Where to go?
Birds of the world be my home,
Trees of the world be my cities,
Map of the world be my unknown neighbour.

Third World

One per cent
Six per cent
Ten per cent
The government beams in pictures and papers,
And squats in printing presses
Capturing its days in stamps
Recording victories,
                    Recording revenge.

Today's poet doesn't read figures,
His tomorrow is now.
                    If he's hungry he blocks the path of the rulers
If he's cold he steals the flag.

The Return of the Veil

Who stuffed the lark,
Stitched fear to its wings?

Who wrapped up that girl in a veil
Like the slamming of a door?

BEIRUT EXPERIENCE

KHALIL HAWI

Lebanon

We were walls facing walls
It was painful to talk
It was painful to feel the distance
Choked by the tragedy
It was painful to talk

SAMI MAHDI

Beirut

So this is Beirut
Lost in the crowd
Staring at battered faces.
So this is Beirut
A woman with many lovers.
When she was shot
The killer left undisturbed.

SA'DI YUSUF

Flying

A cloud fell at noon.
If I were a boy
I'd pick up the cloud
And throw it as a ball
In the garden . . .
And jump in the ball
And tell the dogs:
Bark . . . so I can fly.

Blue

Sometimes I hold the moment's rose –
A fugitive creeping quietly . . .
So distant is the door the chair the statue
The phone the car abandoned round the corner
So calm is the blue woman
In the rose – the moment
Recoiling in the voice
Losing itself in the voice
Until the voice switches off

Exhaustion

We started off
Like two stallions galloping across the earth
And collapsed
Like the sun's shadow
In the corner of a room

A Fighting Position

Might have been a merchant's home
Or a lively widow's home
Or a home in a traveller's mind
The houses geared
In fighter's fatigues
Set up barricades
And disappeared . . .

Where To?

Where's the young man going
On this unusual evening?
A water flask
And a bomb tucked in his belt
And the weapon he never leaves . . .
Is he going to the sea?
This young man . . .

A Room

Has only books
A bed
And a poster
A fighter plane arrives
Lifts the bed
The last book
And leaves its mark on the poster

Water

The lark drinks
The star drinks
The sea drinks
The bird

And the house–plant drink
But the *Sabra* children
Drink the smoke of missiles

Electricity

All at once we remember the village nights
The orchards
And sleeping at eight
All at once we discover the benefits of the dawn
We hear the muezzin's call
The cock's crow
And the village wrapped in peace.

Guns

The guns roar at dawn
And the sea enfolds the city like smoke
The guns roar at dawn
And the birds are frightened
Have the planes come?

In an empty flat
The plants are silent
The vase is shaking

Resurrection

In an unlit hospital
A little boy died of thirst
They buried him quickly
And left confused
Now he opens his wilting eyes
Opens his wide eyes
And digs
Digs deep into the earth

Sabra: A reference to the massacre of Palestinian refugees at the Sabra and Chatila camps in 1982.

Hamra Night

A candle in a long street
A candle in the sleep of houses
A candle for frightened shops
A candle for bakeries
A candle for a journalist trembling in an empty office
A candle for a fighter
A candle for a woman doctor watching over patients
A candle for the wounded
A candle for plain talk
A candle for the stairs
A candle for a hotel packed with refugees
A candle for a singer
A candle for broadcasters in their hideouts
A candle for a bottle of water
A candle for the air
A candle for two lovers in a naked flat
A candle for the falling sky
A candle for the beginning
A candle for the ending
A candle for the last communiqué
A candle for conscience
A candle in my hands.

Hamra: A fashionable district in Beirut.

MAHMOUD DARWISH

Victim No. 48

He was lying dead on a stone.
They found in his chest the moon and a rose lantern,
They found in his pocket a few coins,
A box of matches and a travel permit.
      He had tattoos on his arms.

His mother kissed him
And cried for a year.
Boxthorn tangled in his eyes.
      And it was dark.

His brother grew up
And went to town looking for work.
He was put in prison
Because he had no travel permit;
He was carrying a dustbin
      And boxes down the street.

Children of my country,
      That's how the moon died.

The Passport

They didn't recognize me.
The passport's darkness
Erased the tones of my photograph.
They put my wound on show
For tourists who love collecting pictures.
They didn't recognize me.
Don't let my hand lose the sunlight
For in its rays trees recognize me.
All the rain songs recognize me.
Don't leave me pale as the moon.

All the birds followed
My hand to the barriers of a distant airport.
All the wheatfields
All the prisons
All the white graves
All the borders
All the waving handkerchiefs
All the dark eyes
All the eyes
Were with me
But they crossed them out of the passport.
Deprived of a name, of an identity,
In a land I tended with both hands?
Today Job's voice rang throughout heaven:
Don't test me again!
Venerable prophets,
Don't ask the trees their names,
Don't ask the valleys about their mother.
My face brandishes a sword of light
And my hand is the river's spring.
The hearts of people are my nationality.
Take away my passport.

Psalm 2

Now I find myself dried
Like trees growing out of books.
The wind is just a passing thing.
Shall I fight or shall I not fight?
That is not the question.
The important thing is to have a strong throat.
Shall I work or shall I not work?
That is not the question.
The important thing is to rest eight days a week
Palestine time.
Country, turning up in songs and massacres,
Show me the source of death;
Is it the dagger or the lie?

Country, turning up in songs and massacres,
Why do I smuggle you from airport to airport
Like opium,
Invisible ink,
A radio transmitter?

I want to draw your shape,
You, scattered in files and surprises.
I want to draw your shape,
You, flying on shrapnel and birds' wings.
I want to draw your shape
But heaven snatches my hand.
I want to draw your shape
You, trapped between the dagger and the wind.
I want to draw your shape
To find my shape in yours
And get blamed for being abstract,
For forging documents and photos,
You, trapped between the dagger and the wind.

Country, turning up in songs and massacres,
How could you be a dream, rob me of the thrill
And leave me like a stone?
Perhaps you are more sweet than a dream,
Perhaps you're sweeter!

There isn't a name in Arab history
I haven't borrowed
To help me slip through your secret windows.
All the code-names are kept
In air-conditioned recruiting offices.
Will you accept my name –
My only code-name –
Mahmoud Darwish?
The police and Carmel's pines
Have whipped my real name
Off my skin.

Country, turning up in songs and massacres,
Show me the source of death;
Is it the dagger
Or the lie?

Psalm 3

The day my poems
Were made of earth
I was a friend of the corn

When my poems became honey
The flies settled
On my lips

Earth Poem

A dull evening in a run-down village
Eyes half asleep
I recall thirty years
And five wars
I swear the future keeps
My ear of corn
And the singer croons
About a fire and some strangers
And the evening is just another evening
And the singer croons

And they asked him:
Why do you sing?
And he answered:
I sing because I sing
. . . .
And they searched his chest
But could only find his heart
And they searched his heart
But could only find his people

And they searched his voice
But could only find his grief
And they searched his grief
But could only find his prison
And they searched his prison
But could only see themselves in chains

I Have Witnessed the Massacre

I have witnessed the massacre
I am a victim of a map
I am the son of plain words
I have seen pebbles flying
I have seen dew drops as bombs
When they shut the gates of my heart on me
Built barricades and imposed a curfew
My heart turned into an alley
My ribs into stones
And carnations grew
And carnations grew

Brief Reflections on an Ancient and Beautiful City on the Coast of the Mediterranean Sea

Let her be the mother of this sea
Or the sea's first cry of this place.
Let the one who built her from a wave
Be stronger than the past or a thousand horses.
Let the one who slept in her first rose
Be a girl from Syria.
Why should I care? Why should my times care
About the air that doesn't dry my naked blood?
Why should I care personally
About the sky that doesn't cover me with a bird or smoke?

What makes me leap out of the muezzin's call
So as to pray to the One who taught her his Attributes
And who threw me to the songs?

Let this city be
The mother of this sea or the sea's first cry.
We have to sing for the sea's defeat within us,
Or for our dead lying by the sea,
And wear salt and travel to every port
Before oblivion sucks us dry.
Nothing brings life to this place.

We are the leaves of a tree,
The words of a shattered time.
When the house recedes from the flute, we become the flute.
We are the field that grows in a painting.
We are the moonlight sonata.
We expect from our mirror
Only what looks like us.
We're not asking from the land of man
A foothold for the soul.
We are the water in the voice that calls us but we hear nothing.
We are the other river-bank that lies between the voice and the stone.
We are the produce of the land that is not ours.
We are what we produced in the land that was ours.
We are what's left of us in exile.
We are the plants of a broken vase.
We are what we are, but who are we?
What's the point
Of having a place when we have to pirouette round the earth
Bursting with people like us,
And with the one who'll tumble her down from her high throne
So as to bury us in any place.

Alif, Ba, Ya.
How we used to bite the earth
Like a boy biting a peach stone
Before throwing it like the night thrown
Into the dress of a whore!

Alif, Jeem, Ya.
How we used to enter the light

Like songs entering wheat
And count the martyrs
Like we used to count the cattle!

Alif, Dal, Ya.
We enter the abyss
Without falling, because when people in love sway
The ear of corn holds them up.
Take your time, my song,
So the heart can cleave to the guillotine's blade,
So I can snap the abyss's padlock.

What scars the soul here,
What scars the soul!
Why
Should
I care
About the hand opening dawn's door for morning coffee,
Why should I care?
A lemon is laughing so you can laugh.
The sun opens a rose so you can open it.
Nothing. Nothing. Whiteness.
This whiteness creates another whiteness.
Hannibal's head, or Anthony's ring, a princess's pants –
A stone recording people passing through here,
A stone, or half a stone, recording people's death.
A stone recording I'm only memories, words of memories,
A moon, or halfmoon, following its partner.
The feet of the mountain drink the sea. A sand grouse.
White cats. Rhododendrons elevated by songs.
Decay is real,
Permanence an illusion.
What I've learnt I don't understand
And what I don't understand I grasp it only when it's too late.
A girl splits the dawn with her legs into two beds
And lets in only the unknown, the unknown.
Nothing moves the heart in this place.

Alif, Ba, Jeem, Dal, Ya: Letters from the Arab alphabet.

The beach snakes round the bells on the dancer's waist.
Kings crown the sea with foam.
What is it that's going to end at this moment
In this body?
What is it that's going to begin?
We have devoured the land
And killed the sea in a desperate chase.
What is it that's going to end?
What is it that's going to begin?
A country's grave gives birth to another country.
Crooks pray to Allah
So their people can worship them.
Kings for ever,
Slaves for ever.
No one
Tells Caesar: why should I care
About the crown prince or this country?
Oh,
Why
Should
I care
As long as the soul here
Is the coal in the sultan's braziers!
Nothing moves the soul in this place.
A thousand windows overlook the sea that drowned the Greeks
So the Romans could drown us.
The walls are white,
The waves are blue,
Joy is black,
And the idea a mirror of wild blood.
Put A'isha on trial
Prove A'isha's innocence.
Oh, nothing moves the soul in this place.

Let this city be
The grandmother of the world or whatever she likes, whatever she
     likes.
Why should I care? Every morning

That doesn't come to me first is not my morning!
No . . .
Why should I care? All the winds
That don't break me into distances are not my winds!
No . . .
Why should I care? All the wounds
That don't give birth to a fresh god within me are not my wounds!
No . . .
Why should I care?
Any weapon in my hand
That doesn't return the bread to its grain is not my weapon!

Let the one who built this wall be my grandfather
Or my enemy.
And let the one who named this city be
A knight
Or lover
Or no one.
And let the eyes of jasmine be
The keepers of the secrets since Eve's birth.
Since I'm lost between the stone and heaven why should I care
About the sky
Where I've never flown my flocks of doves,
Where I've never smoked my dreams
Nor caught a moon.
Any branch that doesn't play my childhood games
Nor scratch my hand is not a branch of a tree.
Come what may,
Nothing moves the soul in this place.

The place is the smell, the mystery of the first woman.
Morning coffee opening the window,
The father hanging the sea on the wall.
The place is the appetite:
My first step into the first pair of legs lit my body,
And I got to know my body and the narcissus within me.
The place is the first sickness.
A mother squeezes a cloud to wash a dress. The place
Is what used to and still is stopping me from playing.

The place is the *Fatiha*.
The place is the first year, the noise of the first tear,
The water looking at the girls, the initial sexual pain, the bitter honey,
The wind coming from a song, the rock of my ancestors, my limpid
    mother.
The place is the thing travelling from me to me.
The place is the land and history within me.
The place is the thing pointing towards me.
Oh, nothing lights the name in this place.

Greetings, oh sea in agony.
You, sea that have sailed from Tyre to Spain,
You, sea that are taken from us like a city,
A thousand opened windows overlook your navy blue coffin,
Still I can't see a poet there backed by a thought
Or elevated by a woman.
Sea of all beginnings, where do you go back to?
Oh sea besieged
From Tyre to Spain,
Now the earth is rotating,
Why don't you go back whence you came?

      Oh, who will save this sea?
      The hour of the sea has struck.
      The sea loosens itself.
      Who will save us from the cancer of the sea?
      Who will announce the sea is dead?

Greetings, oh ancient sea.
You, sea that have saved us from the loneliness of the forests,
You, sea of all beginnings (the sea disappears).
Our blue body, our happiness, our soul tired of stretching from Jaffa to
    Carthage, our broken pitcher, tablets of lost stories, we looked for the
    legends of civilizations but could only find the skull of man by the sea.
Our first happiness, our surprise,
Does the sea die like a man within man
Or in the sea?
Nothing moves the sea in this place.

Fatiha: The first chapter of the Qur'an and the Muslim's equivalent to the Lord's prayer.

Once
We're accustomed to travelling
All places become
Foam on which we float
And sway
With the wind
And get used to the whinnies of horses.

Once
We're accustomed to travelling
All periods become
The hour of killing.
We have died many times, we have died many times.
And the priests
Were servants of the sword from the first temple
To the last revolution,
But the man in love worshipped the lily.

Greetings, imprisoned land,
God's punishment within us
Grown into God's little paradise.
Who needs a victim
To notice the sea?
Who needs a turtle-dove
To bring up his boy in a test-tube or a gun?
Who needs a victim
To be the only master of the last days of Rome?
Who needs resurrection
To find his twin murderer without an identity?
Who needs the rest?
Who
Needs
The rest?
Here the land with what's on it and those who walk on it
Is a gun.
Here the land is under Rome,
But the hour of Rome has struck,
Has struck.
Every day is the last day. And dreams are metallic fires.
So greetings, land / victim!

Anyone who travels to the night at night – is me.
Any flute that cuts the field –
A caller and the one to be called but no one calls him – is me.
Anything I like is swallowed by the shadow here.
Any girl who asks me for a quick kiss
Robs me of my soul, my steps.
Every passing bird eats my bread from my wounds
And sings for others.
Anyone stricken by love calls me
So my enemies' butterflies can increase.
Any girl who touches her breasts so two birds can scar my heart
Will shrink away.
Every trunk of a tree touched by my hand loses its clouds
Every cloud landing on my song turns into gloom.
Every land I long for as a bed
Dangles as a gallows.
I love love when love recedes.
I love the white lily
When it withers in my hand and grows in my song. Wait for me, my
    song,
We may dig in this place
A foothold for the soul, for the two strangers who pass through the
    land
But never meet.
Oh, this damned place,
Oh, nothing moves the heart in this place.

We are in such a state.
We are the generation of the massacre,
A nation that lops off their mother's breast,
A nation that slaughters the guardian of their dream
In moonlit nights
Without shedding a tear.

Where is the shadow of the tree?

We are in such a state.
Once we led our own lives,
Now who is it who controls us?

A knight stabs his brother in the chest
In the name of the country
Then prays for forgiveness.

Where is the shape of the tree?

Now we are in such a state.
Have they died so I can sing
Or they can set up a tent for the flute?
Whenever I follow them
A desert opens up for me
And a lark dies.

Where is the house of the tree?

We are in such a state.
The sea cannot take another migration.
Oh, the sea has no room for us.
An idea gives birth to another idea:
The gun becomes
An instrument, not a miracle, not a religion of flowers.
The gun becomes
The guardian of the soul,
And not the servant of rotten twigs.

Where is the trunk of the tree?

We are in such a state.
One is a murderer if he witnesses a murder and says nothing.
They have changed his names,
Replaced my victory sign
With my blood on his hand
And put my eyes in his eyes so I can say I've never seen him.

Where is . . . where is the tree?

We are in such a state.
Now there's no death in our death, the river doesn't begin in the saddle,
    nor lust strain itself to conceal a mountain in an arm, nor does the

dusk of the bronze religion dangle from my song, nor a people line
up for the hell of the great pleasure.

We have wronged you, my people.

We have wronged the plants that conceal you from us.

Now there's no death within us, the rock has no rhythm, there's no
rock in the water incident. Let us go to what is not within us to see
what is not within us. There's no invitation for the people within us.
We walk from one massacre to another massacre. We walk so we can
shout: Hello! Here is the rose. Let us prostrate.

We have wronged you, my people.

People of my song, since God came out of his thought to Jerusalem

There's not a rock on which we can build our voices or prayers to ask
forgiveness.

Now we are in such a state.

Whenever a prophet rises from our victims we slaughter him with our
own hands, with our own hands.

I have the right to speak

And the priest has the right to kill.

I have the right of the birds

And the judge has the limits of the vast horizon.

I have the right to dream

And the executioner must listen to me or open the door to let my
dreams escape.

I have the freedom, the freedom to write the *H* as I please,

And to jump from letter to letter,

And to cut off my hand so as to name my times.

There's no death in a death that shadows me

Or slips into my body like a woman who denies me the thrill of not
having her.

My dream leaves me only to make me laugh

Or make people laugh at someone leading a dream like a camel in a
market of whores.

This death is not death. No. I know nothing about my beginnings,
that's why I dream of being close to the river so I can be the river.
No. I cannot die in a death that has no death.

My soul is a stone

My girl and the dream are stones

I don't want to have any desire for them.

A stone has no colour.

My night is a stone,
My shadow is a stone slipping in between myself and me
My bread is a stone
My wine is a stone
I cannot die in a death
That has no death now . . .

Nothing moves death in this place.

When the Martyrs Go to Sleep

When the martyrs go to sleep I wake to guard them against professional
mourners.
I say to them: I hope you wake in a new country with clouds and trees,
mirage and water.
I congratulate them on their safety from the incredible event, from the
surplus-value of the slaughter.
I steal time so they can snatch me from time. Are we all martyrs?
I whisper: friends, leave one wall for the laundry line, leave a night for
singing.
I will hang your names wherever you want, so sleep awhile, sleep on
the ladder of the sour vine tree
So I can guard your dreams against the daggers of your guards and the
plot of the Book against the prophets,
Be the song of those who have no songs when you go to sleep tonight.
I say to you: I hope you wake in a new country but put it on a galloping
mare.
I whisper: friends, you'll never be like us, the rope of an unknown
gallows!

We Love Life Whenever We Can

We love life whenever we can.
We dance and throw up a minaret or raise palm trees for the violets
growing between two martyrs.
We love life whenever we can.

We steal a thread from a silk-worm to weave a sky and a fence for our
   journey.
We open the garden gate for the jasmine to walk into the street as a
   beautiful day.
We love life whenever we can.
Wherever we settle we grow fast-growing plants, wherever we settle
   we harvest a murdered man.
We blow into the flute the colour of far away, of far away, we draw on
   the dust in the passage the neighing of a horse.
And we write our names in the form of stones. Lightning, brighten the
   night for us, brighten the night a little.
We love life whenever we can.

Horses Neighing at the Foot
of the Mountain

Horses neighing at the foot of the mountain: either to climb or to
   descend.
I give my photo to my lady. When I die hang it on the wall.
She said: 'Is there a wall for it?' I said: 'We'll build a room for it.'
   'Where, in what house?'
I said: 'We'll build a house for it.' 'Where, in what exile?'
We cried and the song leaked.
Horses neighing at the foot of the mountain: either to climb or to
   descend.
Does a lady of thirty need a land to frame her knight's photo?
Can I reach the top of the difficult mountain? The foot of the mountain
   is an abyss or a siege,
And the middle of the road a turning point. Ah, the journey in which a
   martyr kills a martyr!
I give my photo to my lady. Tear up my photo when a new horse
   neighs within you.
Horses neighing at the foot of the mountain: either to climb or to climb.

A Sky for the Sea

A sky for the sea, a sky for the butterfly's daughter to paint a mother, a
sky for a chair.
I come to terms with myself even if jasmine comes too late. I come to
terms with Sunday.
I'll take the river off your hand so it can strip naked, and I'll learn how
the rays become a body.
I'll take my arm off you to seat the last glow as a boy on your hand.
A sky for the sea and a sea for the garden wall. This daylight is my
wedding bed.
The doves alight on the soldiers' stripes, and a girl frees herself from her
lover to snatch a piece of the sun.
Today I love you as I've never loved you before. I remove the foam off
the wave of jasmine.
Is there anything other than peace on earth? Is there anything other than
joy in people? I come to terms with myself.
Do the silver birds die on such a day, does anyone die?

The Flute Cried

The flute cried. If I could I would walk to Damascus like an echo.
The silken are wailing along the coast, vibrating in the shouts that reach
nowhere,
The distances fall on us like tears. The flute cried. Cut the sky into two
women. Cut the road and cut the grouse.
We parted to fall in love. Flute, be gentle, we're not far from the sunset.
When you cry, do you just cry
Or do you cry to pierce the mountain rocks and the apple of love? Spear
of the distant silence that screams:
Damascus, woman, can I love and stay alive?
The flute cried. If I could I would walk to Damascus like an echo.
I believe what I could never have believed. Silk tears heave within us
like a hand.
The flute cried. If I could cry like a flute . . . I would know Damascus.

We Lost but Love Gained Nothing

We lost but love gained nothing
Because you, love, spoilt child,
Smashed the sky's only door and our unsaid words, then disappeared.
How many flowers we haven't seen today. How many streets haven't
    dispelled the grief in the heart of a man in chains.
How many girls whose years have bypassed us and gone to a place we
    could not see to neigh like horses.
How many songs have come to us but we were asleep. How many new
    moons have descended
To rest on a pillow. How many kisses have knocked on our door while
    we were away.
How many dreams we have lost in our sleep while we were working,
    looking for bread in the rocks.
How many birds have flown around our windows while we were
    playing with our chains in a postponed day.
We lost a great deal but love gained nothing, because you, love, are a
    spoilt child.

We Travel Like Other People

We travel like other people, but we return to nowhere. As if travelling
Is the way of the clouds. We have buried our loved ones in the darkness
    of the clouds, between the roots of the trees.
And we said to our wives: go on giving birth to people like us for
    hundred of years so we can complete this journey
To the hour of a country, to a metre of the impossible.
We travel in the carriages of the psalms, sleep in the tent of the prophets
    and come out of the speech of the gypsies.
We measure space with a hoopoe's beak or sing to while away the
    distance and cleanse the light of the moon.
Your path is long so dream of seven women to bear this long path
On your shoulders. Shake for them palm trees so as to know their
    names and who'll be the mother of the boy of Galilee.
We have a country of words. Speak speak so I can put my road on the
    stone of a stone.
We have a country of words. Speak Speak so we may know the end of
    this travel.

ACKNOWLEDGEMENTS

ADONIS (ALI AHMAD SA'ID)

'The New Noah' first published in Arabic in Beirut 1958; this translation first published in *Victims of a Map* (ed. A. al-Udhari) by ALSAQI Books (London) 1984: copyright 1958 by Adonis; translation copyright © Abdullah al-Udhari, 1984. 'The Wound' first published in Arabic in Beirut 1961; this translation first published in *Victims of a Map* (ed. A. al-Udhari) by ALSAQI Books (London) 1984: copyright © Adonis, 1961; translation copyright © Abdullah al-Udhari, 1984. 'The Fire Tree' first published in Arabic in Beirut 1965; this translation first published in *Stand*, vol. 22, no. 1, 1981: copyright © Adonis, 1965; translation copyright © Abdullah al-Udhari, 1981. 'A Mirror for the Twentieth Century' first published in Arabic in Beirut 1968; this translation first published in Great Britain in *Modern Poetry in Translation*, no. 15, 1973, in the USA in *Poetry of Asia* (ed. K. Bosley) by Weatherhill (New York) 1979, in Australia in *The Angus and Robertson Book of Oriental Verse* (ed. K. Bosley) by Angus & Robertson (North Ryde, N.S.W.) 1979: copyright © Adonis, 1968; translation copyright © Abdullah al-Udhari, 1973. 'A Mirror for Autumn' first published in Arabic in Beirut 1968; this translation first published in Great Britain in *A Mirror for Autumn* (ed. A. al-Udhari) by The Menard Press (London) 1974, in the USA in *New Writing from the Middle East* (ed. L. Hamilian and J. D. Yohannan) by Frederick Ungar (New York) 1978: copyright © Adonis, 1968; translation copyright © Abdullah al-Udhari, 1974. 'Invasion' first published in Arabic in Beirut 1968; this translation first published in *Stand*, vol. 22, no. 1, 1981: copyright © Adonis, 1968; translation copyright © Abdullah al-Udhari, 1981. 'The Minaret' first published in Arabic in Beirut 1968; this translation first published in *Victims of a Map* (ed. A. al-Udhari) by ALSAQI Books (London) 1984: copyright © Adonis, 1968; translation copyright © Abdullah al-Udhari, 1984. 'The Bird' first published in Arabic in Beirut 1968; this translation first published 1986: copyright © Adonis, 1968; translation copyright © Abdullah al-Udhari, 1986. 'The Desert' first published in Arabic and in translation in *Victims of a Map* (ed. A. al-Udhari) by ALSAQI Books (London) 1984; this revised version first published in Arabic in Beirut 1985; this revised translation first published 1986: copyright © Adonis, 1984, 1985; translation copyright © Abdullah al-Udhari, 1984, 1986.

ABDUL WAHAB AL-BAYATI

'The Fugitive' first published in Arabic in Beirut 1960; this translation first published 1986: copyright © Abdul Wahab al-Bayati, 1960; translation copyright © Abdullah al-Udhari, 1986. 'An Apology for a Short Speech' and 'To Ernest Hemingway' first published in Arabic in Beirut 1964; these translations first published in *The Singer and the Moon* by TR Press (London) 1976: copyright ©

Abdul Wahab al-Bayati, 1964; translation copyright © Abdullah al-Udhari, 1976. 'The Arab Refugee' first published in Arabic in Beirut 1964; this translation first published in *South East Arts Review*, summer 1982: copyright © Abdul Wahab al-Bayati, 1964; translation copyright © Abdullah al-Udhari, 1982. 'Hamlet' first published in Arabic in Beirut 1964; this translation first published 1986: copyright © Abdul Wahab al-Bayati, 1964; translation copyright © Abdullah al-Udhari, 1986. 'Profile of the Lover of the Great Bear' first published in Arabic in Baghdad 1975; this translation first published in *The Singer and the Moon* by TR Press (London) 1976: translation copyright © Abdullah al-Udhari, 1976.

MU'IN BESSEISSO

'To Rimbaud' first published in Arabic in Beirut 1967; this translation first published in Great Britain in *A Mirror for Autumn* (ed. A. al-Udhari) by The Menard Press (London) 1974, in the USA in *Poetry of Asia* (ed. K. Bosley) by Weatherhill (New York) 1979, in Australia in *The Angus and Robertson Book of Oriental Verse* (ed. K. Bosley) by Angus & Robertson (North Ryde, N.S.W.) 1979: copyright © Mu'in Besseisso, 1967; translation copyright © Abdullah al-Udhari, 1974. 'Traffic Lights' first published in Arabic in Beirut 1967; this translation first published in *South East Arts Review*, summer 1982: copyright © Mu'in Besseisso, 1967; translation copyright © Abdullah al-Udhari, 1982.

MAHMOUD DARWISH

'Victim No. 48' first published in Arabic in Haifa 1967; this translation first published 1986: copyright © Mahmoud Darwish, 1967; translation copyright © Abdullah al-Udhari, 1986. 'The Passport' first published in Arabic in Beirut 1969; this translation first published 1986: copyright © Mahmoud Darwish, 1969; translation copyright © Abdullah al-Udhari, 1986. 'Psalm 3' first published in Arabic in Beirut 1972; this translation first published in *Stand*, vol. 22, no. 1, 1981: copyright © Mahmoud Darwish, 1972; translation copyright © Abdullah al-Udhari, 1981. 'Psalm 2' first published in Arabic in Beirut 1972; this translation first published 1986: copyright © Mahmoud Darwish, 1972; translation copyright © Abdullah al-Udhari, 1986. 'Earth Poem' and 'I Have Witnessed the Massacre' first published in Arabic in Beirut 1977; these translations first published 1986: copyright © Mahmoud Darwish, 1977; translation copyright © Abdullah al-Udhari, 1986. 'Brief Reflections on an Ancient and Beautiful City on the Coast of the Mediterranean Sea' first published in Arabic in Nicosia, Cyprus, 1983; this translation first published 1986: copyright 1983 by Mahmoud Darwish; translation copyright © Abdullah al-Udhari, 1986. 'When the Martyrs Go to Sleep' and 'We Travel Like Other People' first published in Arabic in Nicosia, Cyprus, 1984; these translations first published in *Victims of a Map* by ALSAQI Books (London) 1984: copyright 1984 by Mahmoud Darwish; translation copyright © Abdullah al-Udhari, 1984. 'We Love Life Whenever We Can', 'Horses Neighing at the Foot of the Mountain', 'A Sky for the Sea', 'The Flute Cried', 'We Lost but Love Gained Nothing' first published in Arabic in Nicosia, Cyprus, 1984; these translations first published 1986: copyright 1984 by Mahmoud Darwish; translation copyright © Abdullah al-Udhari, 1986.

BULAND AL-HAIDARI

'The Postman' first published in Arabic in Baghdad 1951; this translation first published 1986: translation copyright © Abdullah al-Udhari, 1986. 'Guilty even if I were Innocent' and 'My Apologies' first published in Arabic in Beirut 1971; these translations first published in *Modern Poetry in Translation*, no. 15, 1973: copyright © Buland al-Haidari, 1971; translation copyright © Abdullah al-Udhari, 1973. 'Conversation at the Bend in the Road' first published in Arabic in Beirut 1971; this translation first published in Great Britain in *Modern Poetry in Translation*, no. 15, 1973, in the USA in *Poetry of Asia* (ed. K. Bosley) by Weatherhill (New York) 1979, in Australia in *The Angus and Robertson Book of Oriental Verse* (ed. K. Bosley) by Angus & Robertson (North Ryde, N.S.W.) 1979: copyright © Buland al-Haidari, 1971; translation copyright © Abdullah al-Udhari, 1973. 'The Dead Witness' first published in Arabic in Beirut 1971; this translation first published in Great Britain in *A Mirror for Autumn* (ed. A. al-Udhari) by The Menard Press (London) 1974, in the USA in *New Writing from the Middle East* (ed. L. Hamilian and J. D. Yohannan) by Frederick Ungar (New York) 1978: copyright © Buland al-Haidari, 1971; translation copyright © Abdullah al-Udhari, 1974.

UNSI AL-HAJ

'Memory' first published in Arabic in Beirut 1963; this translation first published in *A Mirror for Autumn* (ed. A. al-Udhari) by The Menard Press (London) 1974: copyright © Unsi al-Haj, 1963; translation copyright © Abdullah al-Udhari, 1974. 'The Days and the Giants' first published in Arabic in Beirut 1965; this translation first published 1986: copyright © Unsi al-Haj, 1965; translation copyright © Abdullah al-Udhari, 1986. 'Girl Butterfly Girl' first published in Arabic in Beirut 1967; this translation first published in Great Britain in *A Mirror for Autumn* (ed. A. al-Udhari) by The Menard Press (London) 1974, in the USA in *Poetry of Asia* (ed. K. Bosley) by Weatherhill (New York) 1979, in Australia in *The Angus and Robertson Book of Oriental Verse* (ed. K. Bosley) by Angus & Robertson (North Ryde, N.S.W.) 1979: copyright © Unsi al-Haj, 1967; translation copyright © Abdullah al-Udhari, 1974.

KHALIL HAWI

'Lebanon' first published in Arabic in Beirut 1983; this translation first published 1986: copyright © Khalil Hawi, 1983; translation copyright © Abdullah al-Udhari, 1986.

RASHID HUSSEIN

'Lessons in Parsing' first published in Arabic in Beirut 1971; this translation first published in Great Britain in *A Mirror for Autumn* (ed. A. al-Udhari) by The Menard Press (London) 1974, in the USA in *New Writing from the Middle East* (ed. L. Hamilian and J. D. Yohannan) by Frederick Ungar (New York) 1978: copyright © Rashid Hussein, 1971; translation copyright © Abdullah al-Udhari, 1974.

JABRA IBRAHIM JABRA

'After Golgotha' first published in Arabic in Beirut 1964; this translation first published 1986: copyright © Jabra Ibrahim Jabra, 1964; translation copyright © Abdullah al-Udhari, 1986.

YUSUF AL-KHAL

'Prayers in a Temple' first published in Arabic in Beirut 1960; this translation first published in Great Britain in *Modern Poetry in Translation*, no. 15, 1973, in the USA in *Poetry of Asia* (ed. K. Bosley) by Weatherhill (New York) 1979, in Australia in *The Angus and Robertson Book of Oriental Verse* (ed. K. Bosley) by Angus & Robertson (North Ryde, N.S.W.) 1979: copyright © Yusuf al-Khal, 1960; translation copyright © Abdullah al-Udhari, 1973. 'Enough She Said', 'The Harvest', 'The Last Supper', 'Let the Roots Speak' and 'The Long Poem' first published in Arabic in Beirut 1960; these translations first published 1986: copyright © Yusuf al-Khal, 1960; translation copyright © Abdullah al-Udhari, 1986.

MUHAMMAD AL-MAGHUT

'The Noonday Sun and the Shade' first published in Arabic in Beirut 1966; this translation first published 1986: copyright © Muhammad al-Maghut, 1966; translation copyright © Abdullah al-Udhari, 1986. 'The Postman's Fear' first published in Arabic in Damascus 1970; this translation first published in Great Britain in *TR* magazine (London) 1976, in the USA in *Poetry of Asia* (ed. K. Bosley) by Weatherhill (New York) 1979, in Australia in *The Angus and Robertson Book of Oriental Verse* (ed. K. Bosley) by Angus & Robertson (North Ryde,

N.S.W.) 1979: translation copyright © Abdullah al-Udhari, 1976. 'Tourist' first published in Arabic in Damascus 1970; this translation first published in *Stand*, vol. 22, no. 1, 1981: translation copyright © Abdullah al-Udhari, 1981. 'The Orphan' first published in Arabic in Damascus 1970; this translation first published in *South East Arts Review*, summer 1982: translation copyright © Abdullah al-Udhari, 1982. 'Siege', 'Winter' and 'An Arab Traveller in a Space Station' first published in Arabic in Damascus 1970; these translations first published 1986: translation copyright © Abdullah al-Udhari, 1986.

SAMI MAHDI

'Beirut' first published in Arabic in Baghdad 1979; this translation first published 1986: translation copyright © Abdullah al-Udhari, 1986.

ISAM MAHFOUZ

'The End' first published in Arabic in Beirut, 1966; this translation first published 1986: copyright © Isam Mahfouz, 1966; translation copyright © Abdullah al-Udhari, 1986.

NAZIK AL-MALA'IKA

'New Year' first published in Arabic in Beirut 1957; this translation first published 1986: copyright 1957 by Nazik al-Mala'ika; translation copyright © Abdullah al-Udhari, 1986

SALAH NIAZI

'The Thinker' first published in Arabic in London 1971; this translation first published 1986: copyright © Salah Niazi, 1971; translation copyright © Abdullah al-Udhari, 1986.

NIZAR QABBANI

'Footnotes to the Book of the Setback' first published in Arabic in Beirut 1967; this translation first published 1986: copyright © Nizar Qabbani, 1967; translation copyright © Abdullah al-Udhari, 1986. 'I am the Train of Sadness' first published in Arabic in Beirut 1969; this translation first published in Great Britain in *A Mirror for Autumn* (ed. A. al-Udhari) by The Menard Press (London) 1974, in the USA in *New Writing from the Middle East* (ed. L. Hamilian and J. D. Yohannan) by Frederick Ungar (New York) 1978: copyright © Nizar Qabbani, 1969; translation copyright © Abdullah al-Udhari, 1974. 'Morphine' first published in Arabic in Beirut 1970; this translation first published in *Modern Poetry in Translation*, no. 15,

1973: copyright © Nizar Qabbani, 1970; translation copyright © Abdullah al-Udhari, 1973. 'The Ruler and the Sparrow' first published in Arabic in Beirut 1970; this translation first published 1986: copyright © Nizar Qabbani, 1970; translation copyright © Abdullah al-Udhari, 1986.

SAMIH AL-QASIM

'Sons of War' first published in Arabic in Acre 1969; this translation first published as a MenCard postcard (series 1) by The Menard Press, 1972: copyright © Samih al-Qasim, 1969; translation copyright © Abdullah al-Udhari, 1972. 'The Clock on the Wall', 'The Will of a Man Dying in Exile' and 'The Story of the Unknown Man' first published in Arabic in Beirut 1971; these translations first published in *Victims of a Map* (ed. A. al-Udhari) by ALSAQI Books (London) 1984: copyright © Samih al-Qasim, 1971; translation copyright © Abdullah al-Udhari, 1984. 'The General's Property' first published in Arabic in London 1982; this translation first published 1986: copyright © Samih al-Qasim, 1982; translation copyright © Abdullah al-Udhari, 1986. 'The Boring Orbit' first published in Arabic in Haifa 1983; this translation first published in *Victims of a Map* (ed. A. al-Udhari) by ALSAQI Books (London) 1984: copyright © Samih al-Qasim, 1983; translation copyright © Abdullah al-Udhari, 1984.

RIAD AL-RAYYES

'To Taufiq Sayigh' first published in Arabic in Beirut 1975; this translation first published 1986: copyright © Riad al-Rayyes, 1975; translation copyright © Abdullah al-Udhari, 1986.

FU'AD RIFQA

'Setting Off' first published in Arabic in Beirut 1967; this translation first published 1986: copyright © Fu'ad Rifqa, 1967; translation copyright © Abdullah al-Udhari, 1986. 'An Elegy for Hölderlin' and 'Straw Mat' first published in Arabic in Beirut 1975; these translations first published 1986: copyright © Fu'ad Rifqa, 1975; translation copyright © Abdullah al-Udhari, 1986.

TAUFIQ SAYIGH

'What's Next?' first published in Arabic in Beirut 1954; this translation first published 1986: copyright 1954 by Taufiq Sayigh; translation copyright © Abdullah al-Udhari, 1986.

ACKNOWLEDGEMENTS

BADR SHAKIR AL-SAYYAB

'The River and Death' first published in Arabic in Beirut 1957; this translation first published 1986: copyright 1957 by Badr Shakir al-Sayyab; translation copyright © Abdullah al-Udhari, 1986. 'Rain Song' first published in Arabic in Beirut 1960; this translation first published 1986: copyright © Badr Shakir al-Sayyab, 1960; translation copyright © Abdullah al-Udhari, 1986. 'Shadows of Jaikur' first published in Arabic in Beirut 1962; this translation first published in Jacques Berque, *Arab Rebirth: Pain and Ecstasy* by ALSAQI Books (London) 1983: copyright © Badr Shakir al-Sayyab, 1962; translation copyright © Abdullah al-Udhari, 1983.

SHAUQI ABI SHAQRA

'The Storm', 'Children of a Grieved Mother', 'Returning to Granny', 'The Hotel' and 'The Prison's Stream' first published in Arabic in Beirut 1960; these translations first published 1986: copyright © Shauqi Abi Shaqra, 1960; translation copyright © Abdullah al-Udhari, 1986. 'The Fan and the Observatory Dome' first published in Arabic in Beirut 1962; this translation first published in Great Britain in *A Mirror for Autumn* (ed. A. al-Udhari) by The Menard Press (London) 1974, in the USA in *Poetry of Asia* (ed. K. Bosley) by Weatherhill (New York) 1979, in Australia in *The Angus and Robertson Book of Oriental Verse* (ed. K. Bosley) by Angus & Robertson (North Ryde, N.S.W.) 1979: copyright © Shauqi Abi Shaqra, 1962; translation copyright © Abdullah al-Udhari, 1974. 'Miss Lemonada' and 'Fresh Air' first published in Arabic in Beirut 1962; these translations first published 1986: copyright © Shauqi Abi Shaqra, 1962; translation copyright © Abdullah al-Udhari, 1986. 'The Silver Mouth' first published in Arabic in Beirut 1967; this translation first published 1986: copyright © Shauqi Abi Shaqra, 1967; translation copyright © Abdullah al-Udhari, 1986. 'My Arms Became the Month of October' first published in Arabic in Beirut 1971; this translation first published 1986: copyright © Shauqi Abi Shaqra, 1971; translation copyright © Abdullah al-Udhari, 1986.

FADWA TUQAN

'To Christ' first published in Arabic in Beirut 1968; this translation first published 1986: copyright © Fadwa Tuqan, 1968; translation copyright © Abdullah al-Udhari, 1986.

SA'DI YUSUF

'Flying' first published in Arabic in Beirut 1979; this translation first published 1986: copyright © Sa'di Yusuf, 1979; translation copyright © Abdullah al–Udhari, 1986. 'Blue', 'Exhaustion', 'A Fighting Position', 'Where To?', 'A Room', 'Water', 'Electricity', 'Guns', 'Resurrection' and 'Hamra Night' first published in Arabic in Damascus 1982; these translations first published 1986: translation copyright © Abdullah al-Udhari, 1986.

INDEX OF TITLES

INDEX OF FIRST LINES

MORE ABOUT PENGUINS, PELICANS, PEREGRINES AND PUFFINS

For further information about books available from Penguins please write to Dept EP, Penguin Books Ltd, Harmondsworth, Middlesex UB7 0DA.

In the U.S.A.: For a complete list of books available from Penguins in the United States write to Dept DG, Penguin Books, 299 Murray Hill Parkway, East Rutherford, New Jersey 07073.

In Canada: For a complete list of books available from Penguins in Canada write to Penguin Books Canada Limited, 2801 John Street, Markham, Ontario L3R 1B4.

In Australia: For a complete list of books available from Penguins in Australia write to the Marketing Department, Penguin Books Australia Ltd, P.O. Box 257, Ringwood, Victoria 3134.

In New Zealand: For a complete list of books available from Penguins in New Zealand write to the Marketing Department, Penguin Books (N.Z.) Ltd, Private Bag, Takapuna, Auckland 9.

In India: For a complete list of books available from Penguins in India write to Penguin Overseas Ltd, 706 Eros Apartments, 56 Nehru Place, New Delhi 110019.

PENGUIN BOOKS OF POETRY

☐ *American Verse*	£5.95
☐ *Ballads*	£2.95
☐ *British Poetry Since 1945*	£3.95
☐ *A Choice of Comic and Curious Verse*	£4.50
☐ *Contemporary American Poetry*	£2.95
☐ *Contemporary British Poetry*	£2.50
☐ *Eighteenth-Century Verse*	£3.95
☐ *Elizabethan Verse*	£2.95
☐ *English Poetry 1918–60*	£2.95
☐ *English Romantic Verse*	£2.95
☐ *English Verse*	£2.50
☐ *First World War Poetry*	£2.25
☐ *Georgian Poetry*	£2.50
☐ *Irish Verse*	£2.95
☐ *Light Verse*	£5.95
☐ *London in Verse*	£2.95
☐ *Love Poetry*	£3.50
☐ *The Metaphysical Poets*	£2.95
☐ *Modern African Poetry*	£3.95
☐ *New Poetry*	£2.95
☐ *Poems of Science*	£4.95
☐ *Poetry of the Thirties*	£2.95
☐ *Post-War Russian Poetry*	£2.50
☐ *Spanish Civil War Verse*	£4.50
☐ *Unrespectable Verse*	£3.50
☐ *Victorian Verse*	£3.50
☐ *Women Poets*	£3.95

PLAYS IN PENGUINS

CLASSICS IN TRANSLATION
IN PENGUINS

☐ *Remembrance of Things Past* **Marcel Proust**
☐ Volume One: *Swann's Way, Within a Budding Grove* £7.50
☐ Volume Two: *The Guermantes Way, Cities of the Plain* £7.50
☐ Volume Three: *The Captive, The Fugitive, Time Regained* £7.50

Terence Kilmartin's acclaimed revised version of C. K. Scott Moncrieff's original translation, published in paperback for the first time.

☐ *The Canterbury Tales* **Geoffrey Chaucer** £2.50

'Every age is a Canterbury Pilgrimage . . . nor can a child be born who is not one of these characters of Chaucer' – William Blake

☐ *Gargantua & Pantagruel* **Rabelais** £3.95

The fantastic adventures of two giants through which Rabelais (1495–1553) caricatured his life and times in a masterpiece of exuberance and glorious exaggeration.

☐ *The Brothers Karamazov* **Fyodor Dostoevsky** £3.95

A detective story on many levels, profoundly involving the question of the existence of God, Dostoevsky's great drama of parricide and fraternal jealousy triumphantly fulfilled his aim: 'to find the man in man . . . [to] depict all the depths of the human soul.'

☐ *Fables of Aesop* £1.95

This translation recovers all the old magic of fables in which, too often, the fox steps forward as the cynical hero and a lamb is an ass to lie down with a lion.

☐ *The Three Theban Plays* **Sophocles** £2.95

A new translation, by Robert Fagles, of *Antigone, Oedipus the King* and *Oedipus at Colonus*, plays all based on the legend of the royal house of Thebes.

CLASSICS IN TRANSLATION
IN PENGUINS

☐ *The Treasure of the City of Ladies*
Christine de Pisan   £2.95

This practical survival handbook for women (whether royal courtiers or prostitutes) paints a vivid picture of their lives and preoccupations in France, *c.* 1405. First English translation.

☐ *Berlin Alexanderplatz* **Alfred Döblin**   £4.95

The picaresque tale of an ex-murderer's progress through underworld Berlin. 'One of the great experimental fictions . . . the German equivalent of *Ulysses* and Dos Passos' *U.S.A.*' – *Time Out*

☐ *Metamorphoses* **Ovid**   £2.50

The whole of Western literature has found inspiration in Ovid's poem, a golden treasury of myths and legends that are linked by the theme of transformation.

☐ *Darkness at Noon* **Arthur Koestler**   £1.95

'Koestler approaches the problem of ends and means, of love and truth and social organization, through the thoughts of an Old Bolshevik, Rubashov, as he awaits death in a G.P.U. prison' – *New Statesman*

☐ *War and Peace* **Leo Tolstoy**   £4.95

'A complete picture of human life;' wrote one critic, 'a complete picture of the Russia of that day; a complete picture of everything in which people place their happiness and greatness, their grief and humiliation.'

☐ *The Divine Comedy: 1 Hell* **Dante**   £2.25

A new translation by Mark Musa, in which the poet is conducted by the spirit of Virgil down through the twenty-four closely described circles of hell.

ENGLISH AND AMERICAN
LITERATURE IN PENGUINS

☐ *Emma* **Jane Austen**   £1.10

'I am going to take a heroine whom no one but myself will much like,'
declared Jane Austen of Emma, her most spirited and controversial
heroine in a comedy of self-deceit and self-discovery.

☐ *Tender is the Night* **F. Scott Fitzgerald**   £2.95

Fitzgerald worked on seventeen different versions of this novel, and
its obsessions – idealism, beauty, dissipation, alcohol and insanity –
were those that consumed his own marriage and his life.

☐ *The Life of Johnson* **James Boswell**   £2.25

Full of gusto, imagination, conversation and wit, Boswell's immortal
portrait of Johnson is as near a novel as a true biography can be, and
still regarded by many as the finest 'life' ever written. This shortened
version is based on the 1799 edition.

☐ *A House and its Head* **Ivy Compton-Burnett**   £3.95

In a novel 'as trim and tidy as a hand-grenade' (as Pamela Hansford
Johnson put it), Ivy Compton-Burnett penetrates the facade of a
conventional, upper-class Victorian family to uncover a chasm of
violent emotions – jealousy, pain, frustration and sexual passion.

☐ *The Trumpet Major* **Thomas Hardy**   £1.25

Although a vein of unhappy unrequited love runs through this novel,
Hardy also draws on his warmest sense of humour to portray
Wessex village life at the time of the Napoleonic wars.

☐ *The Complete Poems of Hugh MacDiarmid*

☐ Volume One   £8.95
☐ Volume Two   £8.95

The definitive edition of work by the greatest Scottish poet since
Robert Burns, edited by his son Michael Grieve, and W. R. Aitken.